REACHING
MARGINAL STUDENTS

THE NATIONAL SOCIETY FOR THE STUDY OF EDUCATION

Series on Contemporary Educational Issues
Kenneth J. Rehage, Series Editor

The 1987 Titles:
Reaching Marginal Students: A Primary Concern for School Renewal, by Robert L. Sinclair and Ward J. Ghory
Effective School Leadership: Policy and Process, John J. Lane and Herbert J. Walberg, editors

The National Society for the Study of Education also publishes Yearbooks which are distributed by the University of Chicago Press. Inquiries regarding all publications of the Society, as well as inquiries about membership in the Society, may be addressed to the Secretary-Treasurer, 5835 Kimbark Avenue, Chicago, IL 60637. Membership in the Society is open to any who are interested in promoting the investigation and discussion of educational programs.

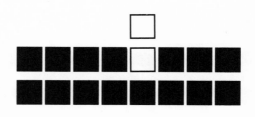

REACHING
MARGINAL STUDENTS:
A Primary Concern for School Renewal

Robert L. Sinclair
University of Massachusetts

Ward J. Ghory
Cincinnati Public Schools

foreword by
Ralph W. Tyler
Center for Advanced Studies in the
Behavioral Sciences

McCutchan Publishing Corporation

ISBN 0–8211–1860–9
Library of Congress Catalog Card Number 86–63773

Printed in the United States of America

Contents

Foreword

Marginality in Schools

Ralph W. Tyler

INTRODUCTION

The term "marginal students" is often used to refer to students who are at the margin of the attention of teachers and other school personnel as they plan and conduct the educational activities of the school. Scant attention is given either to the needs of these students or to their assets. They are viewed, when considered at all, as deviants from the main stream of the school's student body. Although a large proportion of marginal students are from homes where the parents have had little education and have limited incomes, many are from other backgrounds. Marginal students come from well-to-do suburbs and from middle-class communities. Some are from racial minorities, and some are from the white majority; some belong to recent immigrant groups, and some are children of old American families. Marginality arises from a variety of conditions.

There have always been marginal students in American schools and in other school systems throughout the world. Some children were not learning what the schools were expected to teach. The low marks they received from their teachers discouraged them, and most students obtained the same low marks in each subsequent year in school. Before compulsory-attendance laws were passed, parents could withdraw their children at any point in their school careers, and they often did so when their children received poor marks for several years, concluding that their children were not apt at school learning.

After the passage of compulsory-attendance laws, parents could not legally withdraw their children until they reached the end of the compulsory-attendance period—which was twelve years of age in some states and fourteen in others. Later, the age was increased, and in the extreme case of Ohio, the age became eighteen, or the completion of the ninth grade. But keeping children in school who were not successfully accomplishing the learning tasks did not reduce the number of marginal learners. The problem was not primarily one of maintaining school attendance, but was one of finding and developing ways to stimulate, guide, and encourage these young people to learn what schools are expected to teach.

THE EARLIER VIEW OF MARGINALITY

Why was this problem not recognized by the profession and the public until recently? In the first place, the failure to educate a considerable number of children did not create an obvious economic and social problem. Children who dropped out of school could find work on the farm, in the factory, in the store and shop, in the home. As late as 1900, 61 percent of the United States labor force were employed in unskilled jobs; 38 percent were in agriculture, 23 percent in nonfarm unskilled work. Today, less than 5 percent of the labor force are engaged in agriculture and less than 5 percent in nonfarm unskilled work. In 1900 uneducated youth were able to contribute constructively to the economy and few were supported by public or private welfare. Today, most uneducated youth are unemployed. Not only are they unable to contribute to economic production, but many are supported by public welfare programs and some are engaged in antisocial activities of a serious nature. No wonder that the public is now concerned about school dropouts, about youth who cannot read or write or figure.

A second reason for the failure in the past to attack the problem of marginal learners was the common belief that many children were uneducable. Teachers did their work as they had been taught, and if a student did not learn, it was either because he did not have the necessary intelligence or he would not try. Hence, the failure of the student was not thought to be due to the failure of the teacher to stimulate and guide the learner; rather the failure was believed to lie within the student, either in his inability to learn or in his unwillingness to put forth the necessary effort.

The intelligence test movement, which gained acceptance and prestige in the period from 1918 to 1946, gave "scientific" support to the view that many children had a limited learning capacity. Teachers were told by the "experts" not to expect much learning from children with IQs below 90 and not to encourage youth whose IQs were below 110 to plan to go to college. When that concept of intelligence became discredited, the term "aptitude" was substituted to furnish a quasi-intellectual foundation for the view that some students could not learn much. However, in 1903 John Dewey had reported that he found no child who could not learn. He said that the limitations on education are not the educability of some children but the limitation in our ingenuity to find appropriate learning activities that engage the interest and efforts of the child.

A third possible explanation for the lack of attention to marginality in the past is the fact that earlier societies required productive efforts to be devoted almost wholly to the production and distribution of food, clothing, shelter, and other items required for sheer physical existence. In the United States in 1900 only 2 percent of the gross national product was devoted to education, which meant that the resources for education were adequate for only a fraction of the children and youth. In 1910 more than half the children had dropped out before completing the sixth grade, only 10 percent completed high school, and less than 3 percent graduated from college. The resources available at that time would have been inadequate to serve all children, hence those who dropped out could be viewed as helping the taxpayers in their efforts to defray the costs of schooling.

EFFORTS TO REDUCE MARGINALITY

Settlement Houses

Because in the past it was commonly believed that the failure of some children to learn what the schools were teaching was due to the child's lack of intelligence or his or her unwillingness to put forth the necessary effort, few attempts were made to try to reduce the number of failing students. However, the tidal wave of immigration into the United States after the Civil War and particularly in the decades from 1890 to 1910 produced a new situation. New York, Chicago, Boston, and Philadelphia received the largest share of the new immigration, and some local schools in those cities enrolled more children of immigrant families than children of families that had been in the United States for a longer period. Most of the immigrant families did not speak English in the home, which meant that their children had a language handicap as well as the task of adapting to a very different culture. As might be expected, most of them failed to perform their school tasks.

Thoughtful persons, both educators and laymen, who were confronted with this problem did not believe that so many of these children could lack the intelligence required to learn, and they found that most of the children were trying hard to do their schoolwork. Their parents had come to this country from lands where they had little or no opportunities to get ahead, and in many cases they had been oppressed and exploited. They wanted their children to obtain the many benefits of America, the "land of the free." Hence, the parents generally encouraged their children to work hard in school. Some socially minded leaders of that time obtained private funds to found settlement houses in which immigrants, especially their children, could be aided in their efforts to adapt successfully to the new culture. These settlement houses, such as Hull House in Chicago and the Henry Street Settlement in New York, recruited volunteers to help. Many of these volunteers were college and university students who would live in the settlement houses for several months each year so that they could work with the children before school, after school, in the evening, and on weekends. They listened to the children tell of their problems, provided helpful advice, and did a great deal of tutoring. Gradually, these children of immigrant families gained confidence that they were Americans who were doing their schoolwork successfully.

Ability Grouping

Another procedure employed by some schools to deal with marginal students was to divide each class into so-called "ability

groups," in which the children could be taught what was appropriate for their level of ability and in ways appropriate for their
abilities. Since the early studies in the 1920s, evaluative research of
the results of ability grouping have continued to raise serious
questions about this plan, but "tracking" is still common in schools
throughout the nation. Most studies have shown that children
thought to be less able to learn who are placed in separate ability
groups do not do as well on standardized achievement tests as
similar children who are not segregated. Furthermore, children in
the higher-ability groups do not generally make higher scores than
similar children in heterogeneous groups. Social psychologists interpret these results as indicating the principle that differences
among persons in groups stimulate and challenge their reactions,
while homogeneity becomes boring and results in limited stimulation.

Hence, the continuing use of tracking must be accounted for on
other grounds than its help for marginal students. It may be that
the practice has been carried on so long that it is not questioned. It
may be that many teachers believe that marginal students cannot
learn much and hence expect little of them. For teachers of the
upper-ability groups, the task seems easier when few students are
having difficulty in learning. Furthermore, parents of the children
in the upper groups enjoy thinking that their children are superior.
But the current expectation that the school will help all children to
learn may lead to the abandonment of ability grouping and other
practices that promote rather than diminish marginality.

The Smith-Hughes Vocational Program

Following the economic recession of 1912, some educators
noted that many marginal students expressed concern about getting a job. These educational leaders saw a way of interesting these
students in continuing their schooling by offering vocational courses.
John Dewey, in his monumental *Democracy and Education*, had
explained the possibility of making vocational education a liberal
education by helping students understand the function an occupation plays in contemporary society, the problems an occupation
faces in serving society and its participants, the principles that
explain the way the occupation is carried on, and the like. He

pointed out that most vocational training up to that time had not contributed to liberal education because the trainee was taught only how to do the job and was never helped to understand it in its broadest context. These educators joined with influential organizations to press the Congress for legislation that would encourage the development of vocational education in the public high schools. The Smith-Hughes Act of 1917 was the result of this effort. The federal government was authorized to assist the states financially in developing vocational education in agriculture, home economics, and several of the mechanical trades. Later, certain other occupations were included.

As a result of the Smith-Hughes Act, all the states established vocational education programs, and most of the median-sized and larger high schools developed training programs. But, in the 1940s, when the results were reviewed by a commission of the American Vocational Association, it was found that those enrolling in Smith-Hughes programs were not marginal students. These students had been generally as successful in their elementary school studies as those who elected the college entrance program. Few marginal students were being helped by the vocational program.

When this report was presented to the annual meeting of the American Vocational Association, a resolution was adopted asking the U.S. Commissioner for Vocational Education to establish a Commission on Life Adjustment to foster a new program for high school students who were not attracted to the college entrance curriculum or to the Smith-Hughes curriculum. This commission was appointed, and its chairman was Benjamin Willis, then Superintendent of Schools in Buffalo and later General Superintendent of the Chicago Public Schools. But the commission did not make much progress on its agenda. The public viewed "life adjustment" as a term for learning nothing of importance. There was little local support for this approach to helping the marginal student. As a result, few if any high schools have developed what they call "life adjustment curricula," but many schools do offer a general curriculum in addition to the college-preparatory curriculum and the vocational curriculum. Studies of some of these general curricula report that they have not been carefully designed to provide opportunities for marginal students to learn what schools are expected to teach. Instead, they substitute learning tasks that involve little intellectual activity and do not focus on the significant matters that could be understood by drawing on the resources of scholarship.

This brief review of the period prior to the 1960s should indicate that most schools did not see marginality as a serious problem to attack. Marginal students from immigrant families were greatly aided by volunteer programs, but other past efforts to deal with marginality have been relatively unsuccessful.

CHANGING VIEWS ABOUT MARGINAL STUDENTS

Although in 1903 Dewey seriously questioned the prevailing notion that many children lacked the innate capacity to learn what schools were teaching, this early view of the distribution of intelligence was still largely accepted until the 1940s. At that time the findings of centers for research in child development were so clear and the results of the experimental work in early childhood learning centers were so positive that a new view of marginal students began to be accepted by professions that work with young children.

In 1928 Frank Freeman and Sewall Wright reported in the Twenty-seventh Yearbook of the National Society for the Study of Education that they had found the IQs of identical twins significantly different when the children were adopted into homes of adults with differing educational and cultural backgrounds. However, these findings were not widely accepted at that time, for that was the peak period of professional faith in intelligence tests. But in 1940, when George Stoddard and his colleagues at the Child Welfare Station of the University of Iowa reported in the Thirty-ninth Yearbook of the National Society for the Study of Education the results of several thoroughgoing investigations of the different intelligence test scores made by identical twins raised in different environments and were able to relate these differences to observed and reported differences in the learning environments of the homes, professional opinion began a slow change. A few years later, the studies of Allison Davis and Kenneth Eells demonstrated that the commonly used intelligence tests employed a middle-class vocabulary that was different from the common vocabulary of children from working-class families. When they translated the test exercises into the working-class vocabulary, they reported sharp increases in the test scores of these children. Furthermore, they demonstrated that working-class families did not emphasize to their children the importance of taking tests and, as a result, the motivation of these children to do well on tests was low. When the children were offered free passes to the movies if they made high scores, their test scores sharply increased.

Also during the 1940s and 1950s several centers for the education of "children in trouble" reported success in stimulating and guiding school learning of children who were thought to be uneducable. By the 1960s the view of leading educators was that most if not all children could learn what the schools were expected to teach. Students who had been marginal could be helped to become part of the "mainstream."

THE HEAD START PROGRAM

Studies of early childhood in working-class families and in middle-class families had reported several differences that appeared to be relevant to later success in school learning. The language patterns were generally different in middle-class families. The vocabulary and syntax of middle-class families were commonly "standard" English, while the vocabulary and syntax of working-class families, especially minority families, often deviated from "standard English." The experiences with printed materials were different. More middle-class parents read stories to their young children than did working-class parents. The attitudes toward schooling that parents expressed to children were generally different. Middle-class parents would encourage their children to learn in school and to show what they had learned when they got home. Working-class mothers, often harassed by the difficulties of their daily life, would tell their children, "Don't get into trouble. Don't do anything in school that will cause a fuss." Working-class parents' emphasis on passivity was in sharp contrast to middle-class parents' emphasis on active learning. The content of conversations in the home was also different. A typical middle-class conversation about events usually makes clear who was involved, what happened, when or where, and why. A working-class conversation was more commonly free-association without an easily recognized organization of language or a clearly presented sequence of expressed ideas.

These findings led the advisors to President Lyndon Johnson to suggest that the federal government offer support for programs that would provide opportunities for children of the poor to engage in activities that would make up for these lacks in their homes. This, it was argued, would give these children a "head start" when they entered school. Many local organizations, both public and private, applied for support for their Head Start programs. The programs varied widely in particular characteristics, but most of them gave attention to language, reading, and organized conversations as well as provided experiences in social interaction among the children.

After much initial floundering, a majority of Head Start programs demonstrated that the children involved were more successful in their first year in school than were children from control groups.

THE FOLLOW THROUGH PROGRAM

A commissioned evaluation of the Head Start programs found, however, that the greater success of the children in the first year in school did not continue in subsequent years. It became apparent that children require an appropriate environment to continue their school learning. This led to the offering of support for Follow Through programs in which Head Start children would continue to have constructive experiences outside the school that would aid them in their schoolwork. A commissioned evaluation of the Follow Through programs showed that many of the local programs were successful in helping the Head Start children to continue successful work through the primary grades.

TITLE I PROGRAM

President Lyndon Johnson concentrated the major part of his domestic program on helping to create a "Great Society" in which equality of opportunity would be provided for all, regardless of differences in race and income. He appointed a task force in 1964 to recommend policies for education that could promote this Great Society. A key recommendation of this task force concerned marginal children, and Title I of the Elementary and Secondary Education Act (ESEA) of 1965 authorized the expenditure by the federal government of about $1 billion to supplement the local educational resources employed to educate children in schools in which there was a concentration of students from families with incomes of less than $4,000 per year. This was the first time in our nation's history that the federal government was authorized to spend significant sums on elementary and secondary education. Title I was generally referred to as the program for the education of disadvantaged children.

The Elementary and Secondary Education Act was passed so late in the school year that it was impossible for most of the schools to use the funds that year to employ additional personnel. Many schools spent the federal funds for technological aids, such as teaching machines, TV sets, videotape equipment, moving picture projectors, and the like. A great many purchases were made without thought of the ways in which these aids might help in educating disadvantaged children. After this first year, the added funds were largely spent on additional personnel, more teachers, teacher aides, and learning consultants.

The ESEA of 1965 included a provision that a National Advisory Council on the Education of Disadvantaged Children be appointed by the President to give general oversight to the programs that were developed and to see that they were systematically evaluated. As might be expected, very few of the programs showed positive results in the first year. The confusion was not limited to lack of experience in teaching marginal students effectively, but also included some school systems that doubted the possibility of their learning and made little effort to work on the problem. In fact, the council found one school system so convinced that poor children, especially black children, could not learn that it used the federal funds to help support its program for gifted children "so as not to waste the money."

However, in the second and third years more and more local programs were producing positive results. By the fifth year, nearly two-thirds of the programs were working. A national evaluation of

Title I programs was commissioned in 1979 by the National Institute of Education. This evaluation study reported that the average results aggregated for all the local programs were significant and sustained.

This experience with Head Start and Title I programs clearly indicates the probability of success in carefully designed efforts to improve the educational accomplishments of those marginal students from homes of poverty. However, there has been little concerted effort to reach marginal students who come from middle- and upper-class backgrounds. Furthermore, the successful programs have been developed in the elementary schools, and few secondary schools have given thoughtful attention to the needs of their marginal students. What little exploration has been carried on suggests that a combination of improved conditions for learning outside school as well as within is necessary.

CONDITIONS OF SOCIETY TODAY AND IN THE IMMEDIATE FUTURE

Two conditions of today's society make the improvement of education for marginal students a serious problem. On the one hand, the rapid developments in modern society require that persons have much more education today than they would have needed a generation ago to cope with the problems of modern living and benefit from the opportunities created by contemporary economic, social, and cultural institutions. On the other hand, more students are not being adequately educated today than at an earlier time. This is due to several developments. The proportion of children from families with little education has markedly increased since 1950. Parents who have graduated from high school are bearing fewer children than parents who have not gone beyond the eighth grade. Many of the latter parents are not able to provide an environment for intellectual learning in the home.

A second condition is that more mothers of school-age children are in the labor force. In 1940, 26 percent of the mothers of school-age children were in the labor force. In 1980 about 60 percent were employed. Some working mothers are able to maintain an effective home environment for intellectual learning, but many are not. Furthermore, other educational institutions such as the church and youth organizations are reaching fewer young people. Hence, at a time when more intellectual learning is needed, the environment that facilitates constructive learning is more limited for many children and youth.

As the progress of American education is reviewed and the current problems are recognized, the need is clear for comprehensive, carefully designed programs to eliminate or to reduce greatly marginality. The problems are serious. They are with us now. They need immediate attention.

It is against this background of developments that the present volume has been prepared to furnish the basis for planning and action.

1

Perspective from the Margins

American public schools face a formidable charge. First, they must provide free elementary and secondary education for all young people up to age sixteen and to any interested young people through grade twelve. Second, schools are required to provide optimum access to any program for an increasingly diverse student population, which includes many students who have previously been the most neglected and disaffected. Third, a balance of academic, vocational, social, and personal goals has been mandated for all students through a comprehensive program of studies and activities to be made available at each school. Fourth, citizens and courts expect affirmative action to reduce barriers to access or success that might arise from economic, racial, gender, or cultural differences among students.[1] In brief, the fundamental mission of public schools is to provide quality integrated education to all.

Such varied expectations expose a troubling contradiction between the responsibility of public schools to educate all students and the current inability of school personnel (and educators in other social institutions) to reach and teach a deserving population on the margins of schools and society. During 1983–85, when forty-three states raised high school graduation requirements, the plight of students who had not been productive and successful under previous standards worsened. As schools challenged students

1

with more-difficult subject matter and expected mastery at increasing levels of sophistication, few provisions were made for approximately 25 percent of all eighteen-year-olds nationwide who do not graduate from high school. To achieve greater excellence in education, these and other unsuccessful students must be reached.

In important ways, the current direction of school reform lacks the diagnosis required for reconstruction that will be adequate either to the problem of unsuccessful students or to the expectations that the rhetoric for reform continues to promise.[2] Little long-term improvement in equality and quality will be gained by simply intensifying the features of the school environment that have proven problematic to the very people we must assist. Well-meaning attempts to ease disconnected and uninspired learners into compliance with a more "demanding" version of the conditions that drove them to the edge in the first place will not be enough. Instead, the traditional assumptions and principles of education—to which some youngsters adapt better than others—must be reconsidered from the perspective of those we have not yet reached.

The challenge is to create effective conditions for learning for more young people. Educators, however, have become too easily satisfied with not reaching students. Some educators have responded to recent calls for quality with a curious resentment, as if they were trying to protect those students who can learn under present conditions from those who can't or won't. The "Fourth of July" rhetoric about equality and quality masks considerable frustration with the shortcomings of previously touted reforms. There is realistic skepticism now, both individual and institutional, over our ability to adjust present schooling practices to accomplish the unfinished agenda with marginal students. This self-doubt may explain, in part, the puzzling blind spots that permit reformers to implement changes in schools without providing conditions that would enable more children to succeed. Lack of faith still lies behind the unfounded questions about the capability of all children to learn.[3] Even while demanding the best, many educators are closet cynics about the likelihood of reconstructing school environments to create conditions where equality and quality can be achieved for all learners. Thus, the long-range outcomes of this turbulent reform period are still too uncertain to predict.

In this book we argue that sustained attention to the persistent difficulties of marginal learners is one key to a more sensitive and persuasive diagnosis of the problems of contemporary education. The perspective seen by learners on the margins of school environments provides a practical and compelling basis for the reforms we must implement to reach higher standards of learning for all. Our focus here is on school settings, even though family, electronic and print media, peer group, church, and workplace may all interact with school and young people in ways that either undermine or promote educational quality. The troubles many learners experience are not caused solely by schools, but the school is the primary institution that American society has asked to cope with the problem. Therefore, we call for leadership from teachers and principals, even though parents, politicians, community leaders, and researchers must join educators in a coalition for improvement. Our concern here is to develop a perspective from the margins. Unfortunately, this view has not been a major force for educational renewal. Now perhaps this call for attending to young people who have found no way to fit into the schools will be dramatic enough to make us recognize that excellence and extra concern for students on the margins are inextricably linked.[4]

We present the perspective from the margins in nine interrelated chapters that describe the problem of marginal learners in school environments and provide a practical approach for schools to reduce marginality. Chapters expand on crucial issues that are addressed too narrowly or are overlooked in the diagnosis for renewal that centers on learners who are connected to the school environment and ignores those on the fringes—the many who are disconnected.

We begin by asking, Who are the students in difficulty? and by clarifying the variety of unproductive ways marginal students interact with school environments. Too often the students are blamed for their own disconnection. Hence, the school is slow to take responsibility. The reality of marginality is that learners have many different kinds of strained relationships with the school setting. These relationships develop through a series of interactions between students and the school environment that either encourage or discourage learning. The interactive role of the school setting with unsuccessful students must be emphasized from the start, so that conditions in schools and in individuals can be diagnosed. The extent of the marginality problem can be assessed by analyzing evidence of dropouts, suspensions, substance abuse, low achievement, and underachievement. The assessment leads to the sobering conclusion that every student runs the risk of experiencing a temporary or perhaps a permanent disconnection from productive learning in school.

Next, it is important to consider the patterns and steps by which students either become increasingly alienated or return to full involvement in school. Knowledge of how students become marginal permits early intervention and reduces the likelihood that problems will advance to a stage where they become intractable. Awareness of the patterns of marginal behavior sensitizes teachers, principals, and parents to warning signals that become increasingly difficult to ignore. Concerned observers might be more likely to act on their commitment to intervene if they recognize cues that suggest a direction for response.

Unfavorable school conditions and hardening patterns of individual behavior do not readily dissolve, primarily because young people and educators alike often experience pressures that hinder their efforts to change. To be realistic about decreasing marginality, we must analyze the institutional purposes that are served by permitting so many young people to persist in unproductive habits. Researchers on deviance, for example, conclude that people outside norms serve a function in maintaining the prevailing characteristics of institutions.[5] In this book we examine the organizational characteristics of schools that block assistance to learners in trouble. Further, we challenge the misconceived ways of thinking that contribute to the reluctance of some teachers to assist marginal students. Meaningful improvement is possible only when the regularities of thinking and operating are brought to a level of critical consciousness where their benefits or their costly consequences can be considered.

Reflection on the problems students have at school helps us understand the central role environment plays in learning. As John Dewey emphasized, we never educate directly by injecting concepts and draining off attitudes, but only indirectly by designing the environment in which young people act, hence think and feel.[6] The necessary role of educators is to create and to refine continually situations in which learning can occur. This is done by consciously setting up intellectual, social, and physical conditions that stimulate young people to act in productive ways and then to reflect on their experiences.[7] In Dewey's view, then, curriculum planning really involves the deliberate creation of environments for learning.

When we consider from this viewpoint the difficulties many students have with mastering a curriculum, we clearly see that narrow definitions of curriculum have actually hindered reform efforts. For example, restricting curriculum change to selecting new textbooks or reworking objectives misses the larger meaning of curriculum. Learning problems are actually caused by well-meaning teachers who accept the perceived mandate to cover prescribed content, but who never learned techniques to assure that large groups of students with diverse levels of preparation, interest, and skills will learn together.

Before curriculum reform can take place, existing meanings of curriculum must be examined in light of the mission of achieving quality and equality. Too often, curriculum—when narrowly conceived as subjects, topics, worksheets, tests—has come between teacher and student. Teachers, intent on classroom control and accountability for subject matter, can come to view young people as students "valued primarily for their academic aptitude and industry, rather than as individual persons preoccupied with the physical, social, and personal needs unique to their circumstances and stage in life."[8] Adolescents, caught up in matters having little to do with the intellectual functions of school, do not automatically connect their "other lives" to the knowledge and skills that interest teachers most. Teaching and learning too often becomes a detached transaction. When curriculum becomes a disinterested business and the schools become an anonymous setting for both adults and youth, no amount of emphasis on revised curriculum standards will achieve quality and equality. Personal attention, support, and recognition must be revived if conditions for learning are to be renewed.

Partly in recognition of this disconnection between student and teacher, a common denominator in the current critique of education has been an emphasis on the capital role of the teacher. Yet it is striking how quickly an analysis of teaching usually turns to higher salaries, career ladders, and "extra" duties—topics only loosely connected to daily life in classrooms. Looking at teaching from the perspective of the margins brings a different set of problems into focus.

Foremost is the need to develop guidelines for planning and implementing instruction that respond to the difficulties of some learners but do not hold back or limit others. The mission to provide quality integrated education has intensified this challenge for teachers by increasing cultural diversity among students. At the outset of the 1980s, American schools, both public and private, were faced with a shift in the makeup of the student population they were to serve; the proportion of children who lived in poverty and in single-parent homes was increasing.[9] Handicapped children who twenty years ago may never have made it to school are there now, together with junior high boys who two decades ago were pumping gas full time.[10] Nearly 25 percent of all public school teachers in the United States have in their classes students with limited English proficiency (although only 3.2 percent of these teachers said they have the academic preparation or language skills to instruct their students with limited English proficiency).[11] Developing ways to teach large groups effectively in diverse classrooms is clearly one significant instructional problem we must confront.

While preparing teachers to fill the coming teacher shortage is clearly vital, the view from the margins recognizes also the need to explore meaningful collaboration among universities and schools as a means to improve teacher education and to initiate renewal in public schools.[12] It is ironic and disturbing to see how divided those who study schools are from those who run them. Colleges of education are the logical source for technical assistance for educators seeking to solve problems through research and planning. Yet most professors are geared toward providing credit courses for recertification or salary-scale advancement rather than toward spending time in classrooms and teachers' lounges to help teachers solve the knotty problem of youth in trouble.

Before the public accords again to teachers the authority and respect they once enjoyed, teachers will have to reexamine their role in reaching and teaching marginal students. There is considerable truth in Theodore Sizer's image of the teacher as a beleaguered, unrecognized, disillusioned idealist, pressured to compromise standards and repress the capacity for caring. Yoked uneasily in unions, many teachers are misled to support tactics that promise improved teaching conditions but actually make the school less flexible and more rule-ridden. Beset by skeptical parents who often demand nurturance in the classroom equivalent to what they wish they could provide at home, the average teacher feels frequently on the defensive against outside forces. But the heart of the matter is finding ways to reach and teach more students at higher levels of quality within the classrooms that the teachers for the most part still control. To turn schools around, to make further progress toward the ideals of quality and equality, will ultimately depend upon the leadership of teachers that grows from their effectiveness and skill in creating classrooms where all children learn.

Recent research has acknowledged the importance of the principal as an instructional leader for the school unit. It is sad that viewing a principal as a leader should come as much of a revelation. This "finding" is a measure of how far we have evolved from the days when the "principal teacher" possessed almost total autonomy to the present when most principals feel at times like middle managers caught in a complicated bureaucratic web whose strands are tugged in many directions by layer upon layer of administration.[13]

Viewed from the margins, decentralization is an essential foundation of reforms to reduce marginality. Many school systems, however, are reluctant to shift responsibility to the school level, withholding from the principal the authority to make key budgetary and personnel decisions that affect curriculum and instruction. This hesitancy may reflect value conflicts within communities that are not clear about their commitment to educate all children and that may resent diversion of resources or requests for additional funds to meet the needs of learners at risk.[14] Conflicting pressures like these, which converge on decision makers in most institutions serving diverse populations,[15] reduce the likelihood that powers now centralized will be distributed. With their average tenure nationally down to three years, urban superintendents tend understandably to zig-zag around sensitive political issues, leaving the local school principal in the position of reacting to conflicting signals. For principals to be able to effectively convert their school into an institution responsive to disconnected learners, a prerequisite is decentralization that frees building leadership to lead.[16]

Within the school the role of the principal is to articulate the mission of quality integrated education in terms of local conditions and to lead teachers and parents in accomplishing this mission with learners. Unfortunately, there is no single magical answer for the problems each school faces, although this book is an effort to synthesize perspectives and advance principles for guiding decisions for renewal. Each principal is responsible for encouraging people inside the school to take charge of improvement and for bringing in from the community and the central administration the people and resources needed to reach and teach all students. The principal must establish a clear conceptual base for decisions, one that emphasizes the priority the school attaches to helping all students learn. The job then is to communicate, even sell, this perspective. Goal focusing of this sort sets the context for the specific directions each school adopts. Gradually, an attitude of "we can do it" will form behind a clarified school mission.

Another way principals must prepare the school environment for improvement is by providing the support needed for teachers and parents to accomplish the agenda of renewal. Principals can take responsibility for seeing that schoolpeople have necessary knowledge about the path to marginality, about due-process rights of students, about effective instruction in diverse classrooms. Beyond stoking the determination to help more students succeed, the principal may increase achievement by assisting the school community to overcome conceptual and organizational obstacles to improvement.

Viewed from the margins, the involvement of parents, citizens, and students in school planning is essential to fulfilling the mission of the school. Further, the "right way to do business in a democratic society" is to involve people in decisions that affect them.[17] To accompany such decentralization, we call for school-site study teams in which parents, citizens, and students work with teachers and school staff to recommend directions for the principal's final decision. Through such collaboration the school community can keep informed of the progress achieved in reducing the number of students having difficulties.

Unfortunately, other ways for parents to be involved in schools (as audience, volunteers, paraprofessional employees) frequently result in distance and disequilibrium between parents and teachers. Rarely do these groups collaborate with equivalent status and responsibilities on decisions affecting the school or individual children. The lack of parent-teacher-student teams in efforts to increase learning in home and school may explain why so few parents and students become involved. To diagnose and correct the many ways students can lapse from productive involvement at school, procedures and policies for calling into action parent-teacher-student teams must be developed. To tackle a student's deep-seated learning problems, some of which have developed from substance abuse or emotional problems, the people who are closest to the learner and have the most information about his or her learning must collaborate. When home and school and peer group work toward the same objectives by using agreed-upon methods, every child stands a better chance to learn more as part of the team.

Attention to the needs and difficulties of students who are not realizing their potential in school points to directions for achieving quality in education. The perspective advanced in this book will stimulate productive ways of correcting the problems of marginal students. Our attention is to reaffirm as appropriate and possible the mission of the American public school to provide quality integrated education. Schools cannot be made significantly better by making minor adjustments to their present organization or by providing greater excellence only for those in rigorous college-preparatory programs. American public education exists to help all youth learn, including those who are struggling in school. The quality of public schools has to be judged by the performance of all students, not by measuring the performance of those who survive long enough to take the Scholastic Aptitude Test.[18]

Although we are concerned that too often a wrong agenda is followed for improving schools, based on an incorrect diagnosis of problems, our intention here is not to set one agenda or impose prescriptive solutions. Rather our goal is to influence the identification of school problems by developing a perspective from the margins. Quality in education is a process as much as a product. It derives from the ongoing care with which people attempt to bring their young into society. American public schools will always have an unfinished agenda, for it is their mission in a democratic society both to transmit the best of our culture to all children and to prepare individuals for critical and creative social change. Too many young people are losing the chance to contribute to this society. Reconstructing the schools in line with their historic mission remains a prerequisite for true democracy.

NOTES

1. John I. Goodlad, *A Place Called School: Prospects for the Future* (New York: McGraw-Hill, 1984), p. 45.

2. In essence, this point is similar to the "third premise" in Goodlad's study, *A Place Called School*, p. 2.

3. Benjamin S. Bloom, *Human Characteristics and School Learning* (New York: McGraw-Hill, 1976).

4. Willis D. Hawley, "We Aided Schools to End Poverty; Now We Must End Poverty to Aid Schools," *Education Week*, 19 October 1983, p. 24.

5. Robert A. Dentler and Kai T. Erikson, "The Functions of Deviance in Groups," in *Theories of Deviance*, ed. Stuart H. Traub and Craig B. Little (Itasca, Ill.: Peacock Publishers, 1975), pp. 8–22.

6. John Dewey, *Democracy and Education: An Introduction to the Philosophy of Education* (New York: Macmillan, 1916), p. 22.

7. With characteristic wisdom, Dewey emphasized the importance of making each individual a sharer or partner in all group activity, so that one feels its success as his or her success, its failure as his or her failure. See Dewey, *Democracy and Education*, p. 16.

8. Goodlad, *A Place Called School*, p. 80.

9. Hawley, "We Aided Schools to End Poverty," p. 24.

10. Marvin Lazerson, "Remembering Yesterday's Lessons as We Improve Today's Schools," *Education Week*, 23 January 1985, p. 32.

11. Office of Bilingual Education, *The Condition of Bilingual Education in the Nation, 1984* (Washington, D.C.: U.S. Department of Education, 1984).

12. John I. Goodlad, "School Renewal and the Education of Educators: The Partnership Concept" (Discussion paper, Center for Curriculum Studies, School of Education, University of Massachusetts at Amherst, Fall 1986).

13. Ernest L. Boyer, *High School: A Report on Secondary Education in America* (New York: Harper and Row, 1983), pp. 219–230.

14. Harold Howe II and Marian Wright Edelman, *Barriers to Excellence: Our Children at Risk* (Boston: National Coalition of Advocates for Students, 1985), pp. 94–96.

15. Warren G. Bennis, *The Unconscious Conspiracy: Why Leaders Can't Lead* (New York: AMA Co., 1976).

16. Boyer reaches this same conclusion in *High School*, p. 229.

17. Don Davies, quoted in Howe and Edelman, *Barriers to Excellence* p. 101.

18. Edward McDill, Aaron Pallas, and Gary Natriello, "Raising Standards and Retaining Students: The Impact of the Reform Recommendations on Potential Dropouts," Report No. 385 (Baltimore: Center for Social Organization of Schools, Johns Hopkins University, 1985), pp. 30–31. This report proposes measuring student performance on a "full-enrollment model," factoring in the past test scores of dropouts, rather than on the predominant "survivor" model, which includes only the scores of students still enrolled.

2

The Reality of Marginality

To be marginal is to experience a strained, difficult relationship with educational conditions that have been organized to promote learning.[1] Because the curriculum, instruction, and school organization do not contribute readily to the learning of marginal students, these young people can become disconnected from conditions that were intended to foster academic skills and competencies.

Marginal students balance on a thin line separating academic success from mediocrity or failure. If students lean (or are pushed by the school environment) toward underachievement or failure in school, they risk becoming marginal. For the considerable number of students who do cross the line and become marginal, the opportunities for learning and for receiving a quality education are less than for successful learners. Marginal students, then, have unequal access to knowledge and are limited to educational experiences that do not encourage them to learn. Over time, this unproductive relationship with the curriculum of the school limits their life and educational options. Unless the situation of these marginal students is considered, the current educational reform movement will have little impact on increasing equality of opportunity and academic excellence for a sizeable population of young people.

Ralph Tyler helps us understand the link between marginal learners and school improvement. He suggests that when American society was changing slowly and only a fraction of children needed to learn what public schools were expected to teach, improvement in education was not deemed necessary. Many children did not learn much in school and dropped out after a few years. Now this is no longer the case. All students need to learn what schools are expected to teach, but in every school some students are not achieving. These are the students we consider marginal. Answers to the questions of why these students are not achieving and how they can be helped to learn can guide fundamental school reform.[2]

Various types of students become marginal, such as the learner not working up to potential, the understimulated exceptional learner, the one with a long history of academic failure or substandard achievement, and the one suddenly performing poorly despite previous success. Students can become marginal regardless of sex, race, family structure, or economic background. Marginal learners, then, can include "children at risk" from low-income minority homes as well as youth from well-to-do families who are forced to maintain a delicate balance on the margins because they face less-than-constructive circumstances in the school setting. For some the experience of disconnection or marginality will be short-lived. Yet for many the disconnection and resulting deficiencies will be a critical step on a downward path, one that may exact a heavy cost on society as well as on the individual. For too many learners, being marginal becomes a way of life in school.

Schools often permit a significant degree of marginality—that is, disconnection between students and the conditions designed for learning. In other words, schools allow individuals or subgroups to develop and sustain faulty or incomplete relationships with other school members and programs. For a complex combination of reasons (which we will explore in chapter 4), most schools tolerate the existence of a fringe population that is not fully involved in the mainstream of school life. These marginal students learn and contribute only a fraction of what they can and thus use only a portion of their potential at school.

At the heart of making American public education more effective is the simple fact that too many young people have difficulties relating constructively and connecting productively to school settings. This is different from saying that schoolwork is difficult for these students or is beyond their ability. Instead, the emphasis here is on the quality of the relationship between the learner and the setting, on the opportunities provided that allow the student to appreciate and complete school tasks rather than on the difficulty of the tasks themselves. Particularly during this period in which high school graduation requirements and college-preparatory standards are being made more rigorous, it is important to address the more fundamental problem of access to success at school. Significant improvement of public schools can come only if we reduce the numbers of young people who seem unable to succeed with the current means they find available at school.

THE EXTENT OF MARGINALITY

Marginality in school has multiple sources, including students' origins, present school and community conditions, even the students' anticipated futures. Pupils are a product of family and community environments that have predisposed them to patterns of behavior that are more or less functional in school settings. As a secondary socialization agency, the school typically builds on, refines, or causes reconsideration and reorganization of patterns of thought and action developed in the family and community. Although a small percentage of young people suffer from severely damaged personalities or from serious physical or mental handicaps, it is estimated that less than 5 percent of young people enter school with relatively inalterable problems in learning.[3] Students' origins by themselves are seen to account for only a small fraction of delinquent acts, and origins have a negligible impact on students' becoming marginal.[4]

The prime issue related to marginality in school is the responsiveness of the school environment to the variations among students that result from students' previous experiences. For this reason, we consider the school environment to be both a force that contributes to students' becoming marginal and a resource for correcting marginal behavior. Most important, the school environment is alterable by educators. If school environments do not provide a variety of settings and a relatively flexible approach to variations among their students, marginality is more likely to become a serious problem. For example, when schools place a premium on achieving fixed standards of performance under time constraints, some students inevitably will not find sufficient opportunities to learn. Although educators must be knowledgeable about, and responsive to, influences on student behavior from outside the school, in their "own house" they rightly have the most influence on reducing marginality.

Around the ages of eight to twelve, most young people begin to pay significantly more attention to their peers, to various media (recordings, movies, television, magazines), and to local community norms and beliefs. These aspects of life not controlled by school policies or procedures infiltrate the school environment as significant influences on student behavior. The values and role models provided from outside sources and forces also significantly shape the interactions between students and the curriculum and instruction organized for learning. In recent years the school curriculum has been increasingly adjusted to counteract disfunctional messages sent to students by their peers and the community. Yet if there is a wide gap between the kinds of behavior rewarded in school and the norms and values of the homes and communities the school serves, more students are likely to become marginal in school.

Finally, those who view school as instrumental to achieving future goals tend to be less disengaged from school. On the other hand, those who cannot perceive the articulation between schoolwork and their future lives have less incentive to give their best effort to school tasks. When students sense that future opportunities are restricted, their frustration with everyday tasks develops in part because their aspirations seem only dimly attainable.

Marginality is a complex phenomenon arising from many sources and taking many forms. It is important to emphasize the responsibility of the educator to adjust the school environment as much as possible to reduce the likelihood of a mismatch between the school and the learner.

Students can be marginal in as many ways as they can experience unproductive dimensions of an educational environment. Take, for example, the analysis of an environment as containing physical, social, and intellectual conditions that influence learning.

A young person can experience the physical dimensions of an environment as limiting conditions, as when an easily distractible student who needs private space for effective learning is assigned to an open-spaced classroom equipped with tables for groups of children, or when an orthopedically handicapped child cannot take a specialized course because it is taught in a location without convenient access. Social conditions can also contribute to marginality for many students, as when a teacher who is less effective as a classroom manager must continually struggle to maintain control of a boisterous group. Intellectual conditions for learning can also be alienating—both for the gifted mathematics student who does not benefit from extended practice on straightforward problems assigned as independent seatwork and for the ill-prepared student in the next row who repeatedly practices the same procedural error without teacher intervention. As these examples suggest, marginality can be specific to a single situation or can be generalized to many aspects of an educational environment.

One revealing way to estimate the extent of marginal behavior is to conceive of a large group of students who have trouble relating to school settings and who act out their lack of success in inappropriate or unconstructive ways. From this group various overlapping subgroups have been isolated for study. School researchers and government agencies document the extent of problem behaviors emerging from these major student groups, such as students who drop out of school; students with low achievement; students who are suspended; students who avoid school through absenteeism, tardiness, and class cutting; students who use drugs and alcohol. It is important to realize that statistics for the behaviors of these groups are maintained in inconsistent and incomplete ways. Yet we assume these statistics are useful for estimating the extent of marginality, since each behavior category reflects symptoms suggesting difficult and unprofitable relations with school.

Dropouts

Young people under eighteen years of age who have not completed or are not enrolled in any educational program leading to a high school diploma or its equivalent are termed "dropouts." A recent compilation of school retention rates by the National Center for Education Statistics indicates that about 72 percent of the young people entering the ninth grade in 1977 received a high school diploma in 1981.[5] National statistics show that this proportion has remained relatively constant for over a decade, with dropout rates slightly elevated during the late 1970s. Nearly one million young people withdraw from school each year because outside pressures and school-related difficulties make high school completion too problematic. As they face this decision to exit, these young people experience the most intense of marginal relations with schools.

Average dropout rates conceal the performance of the successful schools and districts that reach most students, while they mask severe difficulties in other schools. In some school districts, and particularly for certain ethnic and cultural groups, the dropout rate is more alarming. In six states (Florida, Georgia, Louisiana, Mississippi, New York, and Tennessee) and in the District of Columbia, more than one in three students do not graduate with their classes.[6] In New York City the dropout rate is approximately 42 percent;[7] in Chicago, approximately 43 percent.[8] In the central Appalachian region the dropout rate is 38 percent, and 30 percent in southern Appalachia.[9] Among native Americans, Hispanics, and blacks, dropout rates are consistently higher than for whites and Asians. The differential dropout rates among these groups seriously affect their rate of participation in higher education.[10] Further, since minority groups represent an increasing proportion of the youth population,[11] some researchers conclude that if minority students continue to leave school at the current rate, the number of school dropouts is likely to increase in the near future.[12]

To see these trends in context, it is useful to compare current dropout rates with those from previous time periods. In the 1900s, for example, about 11 percent of all fourteen- to seventeen-year-olds were enrolled in high school and only 10 percent of those who made it to high school graduated.[13] In the 1930s about one-third of the pupils completed the twelfth grade, and in the early 1950s slightly more than one-half of the eligible students graduated from high school.[14] Many features of contemporary secondary school organization still derive from the early twentieth century when the school environment was designed to signal to many students that academic study, college preparation, and school-based vocational skills were not necessary or appropriate for them. Grading policies, grouping practices, instructional methods, and course content made it clear to some pupils that entry to work and family responsibilities without a high school diploma was not only permissible but even advisable. To a degree, teachers' attitudes reflected the same message. In other words, the marginal status of some students was at one time expected and accepted. School was not the place for many students because young people had meaningful alternatives for employment and adult activities outside school.

Today, because skills taught in high school are the bare minimum prerequisites for meaningful employment, the attitudes and practices of the past must be reexamined. Educators experience difficulties in stemming the tide of dropouts despite the increasing importance of skills and competencies represented by a diploma. When we reconsider the dropout phenomenon in terms of marginal students in contemporary times, our attention is directed to those features of the school environment that continue to communicate the invalid and misleading message that some students do not belong and cannot be successful in school. The minimum standard for our democratic society today should be high school graduation for all. The current loss of more than one in four students before they complete high school remains the most dramatic evidence of widespread marginality in schools. Reduction of this high dropout rate is a priority for school improvement.

Low Achievement and Underachievement

The academic achievement of marginal students is often of two sorts: low achievement (below-average performance compared to grade level or group norms) and underachievement (academic performance less than one's capability). Either of these conditions can be temporary (as when a child experiences a sudden dip in achievement) or lasting. Few school districts are eager to publish such data, so researchers can at best estimate the percentage of students who are marginal because of poor achievement.

Norm-referenced tests are calibrated so that approximately 23 percent of the students nationwide achieve in a "below-average" category. However, the skills and content measured are loosely

Table 2–1
Percentage Passing Initial Competency Test Performances by Students' Race

State	Test Date	Grade Tested	Reading/ Communication		Mathematics		Combined	
			Black	White	Black	White	Black	White
California	1980	12	–	–	–	–	65	85
Florida	1978	11	89	99	40	83	–	–
North Carolina	1979	11	79	97	73	95	–	–
Virginia	1981	10	–	–	–	–	87	97

Source: Robert C. Serow, "Effects of Minimum Competency Testing for Minority Students: A Review of Expectations and Outcomes," *Urban Review* 16, no. 2 (1984): 67–75.

associated with each school district's curriculum, so the scores are an imperfect indicator of actual student achievement. In the late 1970s and early 1980s increased interest in criterion-referenced tests tied directly to school curricula began to produce better data on the grade-level performance of children.

Minimum competency tests related to high school graduation are helpful in estimating the extent of marginality in two ways. First, the results on the initial generation of competency tests are useful for deriving general estimates of the percentage of children achieving below the minimal standards necessary for success at their grade level. Second, test results highlight substantial discrepancies between the test performances of black and white classmates.[15]

Most evidence of the actual outcomes of competency testing remains fragmentary and unpublished. Table 2–1 presents data from testing in states that use diploma denial as a sanction for test failure. Between 1 percent and 15 percent of the white students still in high school could be judged seriously marginal because they lack minimal skills. Between 11 percent and 60 percent of the black

Table 2–2
Percentage of Students at or Above Scale Points on the NAEP Reading Achievement Scale, 1984

Age	Rudimentary (150)	Basic (200)	Intermediate (250)	Adept (300)	Advanced (350)
9	94	64	18	1	0
13	100	94	60	11	0
17	100	99	84	39	5

Source: "Reading Performance Trends, 1971–1984: Their Significance," NEAPgram 4 (Princeton, N.J.: National Assessment of Educational Achievement, Fall 1985).

students did not reach minimal mastery levels in reading or mathematics. State by state, a 10 percent to 20 percent discrepancy range between the performance of white and black students was evident. The performance of students on initial competency tests is an imperfect indication of how much marginality is related to low achievement in part because test scores tend to improve substantially for many students upon retesting. However, if a student has been promoted for years in a school system but cannot attain academic standards considered minimal, the student must be considered marginal.

One meaningful measure of average, as opposed to minimal, student skills nationally comes from the National Assessment of Educational Progress (NAEP), which has sampled scores on reading tests in 1971, 1975, 1980, and 1984. Their reading scale of scores from 0 to 500 places students at rudimentary, basic, intermediate, adept, and advanced levels of performance. Table 2–2 summarizes the findings from 1984. While virtually all of America's thirteen- and seventeen-year-old students have basic reading skills, approximately 36 percent of the nine-year-olds and 40 percent of the thirteen-year-olds are likely to be having trouble with their school reading materials. By age seventeen, 84 percent of those still in school have intermediate reading skills and can work with basic textual materials. However, only 5 percent of America's seventeen-year-olds still in school have the advanced skills needed to handle specialized or professional materials, and only 39 percent can work successfully with relatively complicated literary and informational material. On average, seventeen-year-old black and Hispanic students still read only about as well as thirteen-year-old white students. By NAEP measures, since 1970 overall pupil performance improved in reading at all age levels, with the performance of black and Hispanic students improving at a much greater rate than the performance of white students. Despite this encouraging finding, it is clear that inadequate reading skills are likely to be among the important reasons many students become marginal.

Preliminary results from the NAEP's 1983–84 assessment of writing achievement provided a multifaceted analysis of the writing skills of eleventh-grade students, summarized here in Table 2–3. A variety of writing tasks were assigned (informative, analytic, persuasive, narrative, descriptive). On all but the newspaper report (based on a list of facts about a haunted house) and the imaginative narrative (a ghost story), more than two-thirds of the papers were judged as inadequate or worse. It is sobering to conclude from the results of this national study that as many as two-thirds of the seventeen-year-olds still in school run the risk of becoming marginal due to inadequate writing skills.

Unfortunately, the NAEP has not developed scales to categorize student achievement levels in mathematics, science, and political knowledge and attitudes. Instead, trends are reported in mean percentage scores that are not as useful for determining how many pupils are likely to be marginal due to low achievement.

Tests that measure students' mastery of grade-level standards are also being developed by states and school districts. In Pennsylvania, for example, 32 percent of the approximately 350,000 public school students in grades three, five, and eight who took a new statewide test in 1984 failed to pass the cut-off scores.[16] In New York City, Atlanta, Dade County (Florida), and Philadelphia, promotion to the next grade level is being tied to test scores and quantifiable criteria other than age. Officials there are expecting the percentage of students being retained in grades one to eight to

Table 2–3
NAEP's 1983–84 Writing Assessment Results for Grade 11, in Percent

Task	Non-Ratable	Unsatis-factory	Marginal	Satis-factory	Very Good	Marginal or Less
Informative newspaper report	1	12	27	55	5	39
Short analytic essay	1	14	61	22	2	75
Persuasive letter 1	2	8	69	19	2	77
letter 2	1	32	40	25	3	72
Imaginative narrative	2	3	42	48	5	45
Imaginative description	1	30	50	17	2	80

Source: Ina Mullis, "Writing Achievement and Instruction Results from the 1983–84 NAEP Writing Assessment" (Paper given at the annual meeting of the National Council of Teachers of English, Philadelphia, 1985).

double or triple when promotion policies based on academic standards go into effect. For example, Table 2–4 shows one midwestern urban school district's promotion rates, demonstrating that less retention typically occurs in the early grades. Also, the data imply that achievement of essential skills is likely more of a factor for retention in later grades.

After first grade relatively small percentages of children are

Table 2–4
One Urban School District's Retention of Students by Grade, 1984–85

Grade	Retention Rate (by percentage)	Grade	Retention Rate (by percentage)
K	0.5	7	12.3
1	13.3	8	10.0
2	4.8	9	27.6
3	2.8	10	20.6
4	2.6	11	9.8
5	1.9	12	15.9
6	1.5		

Source: Communication from Joseph Gastright, Director, Evaluation Branch, Cincinnati Public Schools, 1985.

retained in elementary school. One reason is that repeating the same or a similar instructional program does not lead to a significant improvement in achievement. More of the same is not the answer. Another reason is that children's social and attitudinal development is improved if they advance with their age-mates. For these less successful elementary students, however, interventions for correcting low achievement appear to be inadequate. The students move on carrying the baggage of inadequate skills. But when socially promoted students with low entry skills and poor work habits reach junior high school, nonpromotion rates skyrocket. Junior high school environments focus more on subject-matter mastery and preparation for graduation requirements. Thus the poorly prepared students face highly frustrating and discouraging conditions. Nonpromotion, coupled with the students' diminishing confidence in their ability to master the skills that they should have learned long before, can lead these youngsters to becoming marginal and too often to making the decision to drop out or tune out.

It is no simple matter for school or state officials to administer criterion-referenced tests and expect near grade-level performance by students before their promotion to the next grade. According to the National Black Child Development Institute, 43 percent of black males aged fourteen to seventeen and 38 percent of black females in the same age group are currently not achieving at grade level.[17] While comparable statistics are not available, it is reasonable to suggest that achievement below grade level is a serious problem for large numbers of other ethnic and racial groups, and also for white students, particularly those coming from poor homes. Follow-up instructional programs that would allow nonpromotion to lead to a meaningful opportunity to gain needed skills would have to be implemented for over one-third of the pupils in this country if retention is to be more than a punishment and a discouraging signal.

The city school district in Philadelphia provides a case in point. A study prepared in 1984 for the superintendent's committee on student promotion predicted that if students in grades one through eight were required to pass tests at a minimal level before they could be promoted, the district would have to retain 23.2 percent of these students in 1985—up from 8.7 percent in 1984. If the cutoff were set high enough to ensure that students met grade-level standards, the district would have to retain 38.4 percent of the students in grades one through eight.[18] These estimates suggest that an extensive amount of low achievement and underachievement has been masked by the policies of social promotion and norm-referenced testing.

Low achievement and underachievement are by no means restricted to students in the cities, to "disadvantaged" students, to students from economically poor homes, and to students with previously deficient achievement. In American public schools, marginal behavior can emerge unexpectedly—for a gifted student, for a student whose teacher was changed, for learners whose families become disrupted. It is difficult to predict that an individual will not become marginal. In a 1984 study of nonpromotion at grades nine and ten in the Cincinnati Public Schools, achievement scores, attendance data, previous failure record, suspensions, race, sex, socioeconomic status, and student self-report data were collected for 2,424 students, of whom 423 (17.5 percent) were subsequently not promoted to the next grade. Using a combination of all these factors, discriminant analysis accurately placed 97 percent of the students in the passing group. However, when applied to the failing students, the same set of variables also predicted that 83 percent of them should have passed! In other words, the failing group looked very much like the passing group.[19]

Marginal standing is a concern even with highly able students, who are normally considered to be at the opposite extreme from those who are not being promoted. Estimates of underachievement among the most able have ranged from 15 percent to 50 percent.[20] Lewis Terman's 150 "less successful" students included about one-quarter of his gifted subjects.[21] Jane Raph estimates that about one-half of the top 10 percent in IQ do not prepare themselves for the high-level pursuits they are capable of performing.[22] A two-year study of delinquency in suburban settings found that 18 percent of those who entered the juvenile justice system were intellectually gifted.[23] These estimates underscore our view that many different types of students can become marginal.

Again we stress that marginal achievement is in a major way a function of the individual's relationship to learning conditions in classrooms and schools. In some settings, students considered low achievers attend school regularly, try hard, cooperate in the classroom, and get decent grades and improved test scores because they are learning and progressing. Some students with high achievement test scores do not attend school regularly and are not motivated to complete course requirements; thus they do not achieve to capacity, or they fail. Conscientious parents monitor their children's learning situation in all their classes, since they realize that any student is vulnerable to being placed in settings where he or she cannot readily perform to full capacity without direct assistance and support. The sober truth about marginal achievement is that approximately 40 percent of the nation's pupils perform below grade level, and that incalculable numbers of children with previous grade-level or above-average achievement scores do not perform to their capability each year. This estimate is in line with the findings of other scholars who are concerned about public schools providing appropriate educational experiences for students who are currently marginal. Specifically, the results of the study *Barriers to*

Excellence: Our Children at Risk suggest that marginal students are not a fringe population but are an ill-served majority of students.[24]

Suspensions

The disciplinary tool of short-term suspension from school is designed to be used as a punishment for behavior that deviates dramatically from school norms. This behavior is often characteristic of marginal students. Suspensions generally occur when a crisis is reached, usually after a series of related disciplinary incidents have occurred. As such, suspension rates provide a means to estimate the frequency of serious unconstructive conduct that is likely to be practiced by students who are at odds with the educational environment.

Proponents of suspensions say such discipline protects the safety and interests of the school community, reinforces the authority of school staff, gains the attention and cooperation of parents, and helps students reflect on their own conduct. However, suspensions are criticized for alienating the child and family, for not serving the needs of youth, for teaching the wrong lessons, and for failing to protect the interests and rights of the individual.[25] In light of the considerable evidence that suspensions are sometimes administered in capricious and discriminatory ways, the rate of suspension can be regarded as a somewhat unreliable, but nevertheless revealing, measure of the extent of student marginality related to severe behavior problems.

In 1972–73 the Office of Civil Rights conducted for the first time a national survey of school suspensions, collecting data from 50 percent of the total enrollment in American public schools and 90 percent of all minority students. They estimated that 8 percent of all secondary pupils and 1 percent of all elementary pupils were suspended that year.[26] Secondary minority students were found to be suspended in rates disproportionate to the number of minority children enrolled in school. For example, one in every eight black children was suspended, compared to one in every sixteen white children. These findings were corroborated by a Children's Defense Fund study[27] and Southern Regional Conference study[28] conducted during the same time period.

More-recent data indicate that the discriminating nature of suspension persists and rates of suspension remain high. Unfortunately, analyses based on the 1980 Office of Civil Rights survey released in 1982 combine elementary and secondary suspension rates, which results in lower overall figures than reported above. For example, 4.5 percent of white students were suspended at least once, 9.9 percent of black students, 4.9 percent of Hispanic students, and 5.4 percent overall.[29] Mean suspension rates can also mask the distribution across states and school districts. For example, in Ohio during the same school year, overall suspension rates were higher than national rates: 5.1 percent of white students were suspended, 12.8 percent of black students, 6.3 percent of Hispanic students, and 6.1 percent overall. About 90 percent of these suspensions were at the secondary level. Further, while an overall suspension rate of less than 4 percent was common in about half of the school districts in Ohio, in 10 percent of the districts more than 9.5 percent of all students were suspended.[30] In short, marginality related to student suspensions varies across school districts and across racial and cultural groups.

It is likely that differential treatment of minority students is not due to unequal treatment by the principal or the administrator responsible for discipline. Rather, it may be due to the referral process, which depends on judgments by individual staff members.[31]

Those who analyze the reasons for suspension tend to agree that treatment of different racial groups is equal in cases of serious misconduct. But rates of suspension vary most by race in cases depending upon subjective judgment, such as where the violation is unclear (defiance of authority, disrespectful conduct), where the gravity of the misbehavior can be questioned (play fighting), or where the exclusion may depend upon a teacher's or an administrator's tolerance level (chronic tardiness, truancy).[32] For example, one study found that most of the discipline problems involving black males stemmed from "friction offenses"—conflicts caused by differences in values, style, and culture, including ways of speaking, acting, or showing respect.[33] For this reason, overall rates of suspension tend to increase in newly desegregated situations.[34]

The evidence for gender and social-class discrimination in suspensions is less clear-cut. The Office of Civil Rights only recently began collecting information about the gender of suspended students. In 1980, 8 percent of all elementary and secondary school male students were suspended, compared to 3.8 percent of female students. At issue, however, is whether the gender differences in suspension rates represent differences in behavior or discrimination in the use of discretionary authority for suspension.[35] Neither the Office of Civil Rights nor any state governmental agency has collected information regarding school suspension and social class. A 1974 Children's Defense Fund study, however, found that children were more likely to be suspended if their families were poor.[36] This raises the question of whether minority suspensions may be less of a race than a poverty problem. More research is needed on this topic.

Indicators nationally show that the use of student suspension as a disciplinary tool is increasing. For example, in Illinois 5.6 percent of the public high school population was suspended at least once in 1970; by 1980 the rate had risen to 14.4 percent.[37] At the high school level at least one in twelve students overall, and one in eight black students, currently reaches a point of such difficulty relating to school that he or she is temporarily suspended.

Avoidance

Marginal behavior characterized by school avoidance (truancy, class cutting, excessive tardiness) is also difficult to estimate reliably. Data collected by school districts and government agencies are not standardized and are difficult to retrieve. Nevertheless, the human tendency to avoid problematic and frustrating situations makes school avoidance a useful symptom of marginal student behavior. Moreover, the amount of avoidance gives a sense of the extent of marginal conduct.

Absenteeism for unacceptable reasons is termed "truancy." The exact level of absenteeism that indicates a need for concern is not well defined. One rule of thumb is that a group absence rate of about 5 percent can be expected under normal conditions and for legitimate reasons. [38]

In a study of student attendance in Ohio public schools, average attendance rates remained relatively stable between 1971 and 1983. For the 1982–83 school year, aggregate elementary school attendance in Ohio was 94.9 percent; for junior high schools, 92.3 percent; and for high schools, 91.5 percent. At the elementary school level, 63.8 percent of the districts met the expected absence rate of 5 percent. At the junior high school level, 32 percent met the criterion, while at the secondary school level only 12.5 percent of the districts had less than 5 percent absence. The average rate of absenteeism of at least eighty-seven districts (14 percent) at the secondary school level was two to three times greater than the 5 percent criterion.[39]

Because absence from school may be linked to failure in school, this symptom of marginal status is an immediate concern. The long-term consequences of truancy are also serious. For example, a review of the literature on truancy indicated it was the childhood symptom that most reliably predicted an elevated rate of adult deviant behavior.[40] Particularly for secondary students in selected districts, the truant is clearly a marginal person who is acting to avoid experiencing an unproductive relationship with school.

The question of marginal status in school comes into greater focus when the issue of punishment for avoiding class is probed further. For example, in one survey of 1,500 students and 225 teachers in six high schools, most students (62.5 percent) reported they were not caught for class cutting. Of those who were caught, about half (57.4 percent) reported receiving a "meaningful" punishment for the offenses (detention, parent conference, suspension), while the rest (42.6 percent) received mild or no punishment (incident ignored, verbal reprimand, warning).[41]

Thus, several issues become apparent for deviant behavior like skipping school or class that is likely linked with other marginal behaviors. High percentages of students who miss school (40 percent in this sample) are tempted to risk more-serious deviant acts in school. Further, there is lack of agreement about what the rules ought to be, leaving individual teachers and administrators to establish their own individual codes and expectations. This disparity in behavioral standards among classrooms and schools is widely documented.[42] Indeed, a significant percentage of teachers apparently employ a "sliding rule" system, in which rules are not spelled out clearly from the start but are made up in response to emerging events. Finally, when a rule is broken there is lack of agreement about what should be done with the rule breaker, leaving it up to the individual teacher to decide whether or not to seek punishment of the student.

The treatment of students differs most at the stage when a teacher decides what to do with a student who breaks rules. The level of concern a teacher conveys to an administrator may affect the way a student is eventually treated. Here we find that minority students and students from poorer homes are disproportionately sent to the principal's office for punishment. Teachers apparently view these students as potentially more disruptive and as requiring more discipline, leaving the students feeling they were singled out.

With little agreement on rules and consequences for breaking rules, the probability that students will be evaluated and responded to differently for the same type of behavior increases. Thus, it takes more than breaking a rule to become marginal. Marginal status is an ascribed status in school, a matter of social definition and response with concomitant student reactions. Students do not automatically attain marginal status when they commit certain kinds of unacceptable acts. A student can become marginal when authority figures determine that the student's behavior deserves sanctions that limit opportunities for continued full involvement on the same terms as other students. While some students respond by acting to remove this stigma, many others come to integrate this negative view into their perceptions of themselves. Sometimes they act to perpetuate or live up to this emerging identity. If an observer were to spend a few days in a school administrator's office, it would become clear which students are locked into a pattern of repeated discipline or academic difficulties arising from avoidance. Clearly, patterns of student behavior, academic performance, and the authority's response to truancy can develop into cycles that tend to intensify rather than to resolve the problems of marginal students who are at risk because of their avoidance behavior.

Drug Use

Illicit drug use, another possible key symptom of marginal status, is for many students a symbol of their independence from home, school, and society. Drugs are often used by marginal students both to relieve the tension produced by academic difficulty and to gain acceptance into student subcultures that sanction deviant behavior. Students' troubles in school that arise from their using drugs provide another example of the way marginal status can be temporary (experimentation or selective use) or perhaps permanent (psychological dependence, physical addiction). The progressive nature of chemical dependency also illustrates the way some marginal students go through stages of increasing intensity of marginality, leading to disconnection from the school setting.

It is now more widely understood that chemical dependency is a progressive disease that causes the user to worsen physically, spiritually, emotionally, and psychologically. The user goes through four stages as this progressive disease develops: (1) learning about the drug-induced mood swing; (2) seeking the mood swing; (3) becoming preoccupied with the mood swing; (4) using chemicals to feel normal. [43]

At stage 1 the experimenter learns that chemicals can provide temporary mood swings in the euphoric direction of "feeling good." Through practice, the experimenter learns to control the degree of the mood swing by regulating his or her intake of the chemical. The experimenter can discontinue use or can progress to regular use.

At stage 2 the chemical user seeks the mood swing in social or recreational situations, using the chemical at "acceptable" times and places. The user continues to control the intensity and outcome of chemical experiences and may occasionally suffer physical pain (hangover) from an overuse of the chemical but little emotional pain (guilt). Most users stay in this second, or social, phase.

The National Institute on Drug Abuse found in its annual survey of drug use among high school seniors that the majority of high school seniors in the class of 1983 had reached the stages of experimental and social drug use. Nearly all young people (93 percent) had tried alcohol by the end of their senior year, and the great majority (69 percent) had used it in the prior month. At least 57 percent of seniors had experimented with marijuana at some time, while 27 percent reported using it in the prior month. Fully 40 percent of the 1983 seniors reported having used illicit drugs other than marijuana and alcohol (such as amphetamines, cocaine, hallucinogens, and inhalants).[44]

The risk of serious marginal behavior arises when a user advances to the third stage of chemical use, becoming a preoccupied user. At this stage getting "high" becomes a priority in the person's life. Due to this preoccupation, behavior worsens; a person's clothing, appearance, and language openly identify the individual as a "druggie." Straight friends are dropped. The preoccupied user begins to experience recurring loss of control over chemical use; he or she may get high in class, skip school, or develop increased but gradually unpredictable tolerance to the chemical. The disease can be the source of the marginal behavior in school, but the disease becomes a life-style that persists due to ineffective and dissatisfying relations between the user and his or her school and community environments. At this stage negative feelings about the self are typically not identified and therefore are not solved, resulting in growing chronic emotional stress. A delusional memory system prevents the user from acknowledging the severity of his or her own condition. Without full awareness, the preoccupied user finds his or her whole life deteriorating.

At stage 4 a user must take chemicals to feel normal. Blackouts occur more frequently and physical addiction can occur. Paranoid thinking appears. Guilt, remorse, shame, and anxiety are chronically present. The user's self-worth erodes, and suicidal thoughts become frequent. The risk of marginal behavior in school is greatest for young people at stage 3 or 4 of chemical dependency.

In the survey of the National Institute on Drug Abuse, daily drinking and daily marijuana use were each estimated at 5.5 percent of students (one in eighteen students). Binge drinking (at least five or more drinks in a row on at least one occasion in the prior two weeks) was estimated at 43 percent of all students (two out of five students). One in six students (17 percent) indicated that they had smoked marijuana daily or almost daily in the previous one-month period. The percentages of students using other drugs in the prior month period was 9 percent for amphetamine use, 6.5 percent for cocaine use, and 3.8 percent for use of hallucinogens.[45]

The danger of marginality in school related to illicit drug and alcohol use is present for students in all ranges of academic ability.[46] Initial experimentation with alcohol and marijuana occurs well before tenth grade for most students.[47] School might be the place where drugs are purchased, where drug exploits are recounted, where drug life-styles are reinforced. Data on drug use indicate the dramatic peril chemical dependency poses for the physical, emotional, and academic adjustment of young people. Experimenters and social users may or may not be marginal in school, but preoccupied and dependent users usually are at high risk of becoming marginal. Chemical dependency is a progressive disease, and the majority of high school seniors have entered its preliminary stages. Thus, data on drug use confirm the sobering fact that most secondary students are at risk of developing unforeseen problems in relating to school and hence are likely to experience learning difficulties.

SUMMARY

The reality of marginality, then, is that nationwide one in four students drop out of school before graduation and nearly one in two students do not graduate in certain locations and among certain ethnic groups. The achievement of minority students still lags significantly behind that of white students, despite a decade of gains. Up to 40 percent of all junior high students probably have trouble with their reading materials. As many as two-thirds of the seventeen-year-olds still in school run the risk of becoming marginal due to inadequate writing skills. About one-third of all pupils achieve below grade level. One in twelve secondary students gets suspended from school. One in six students smoked marijuana continually for at least a month some time during high school. No doubt, these varied groups and different categories overlap in many ways. Nevertheless, this discouraging, unrelenting refrain of evidence symptomatic of students who become marginal dramatizes the necessity to learn more about how students reach the point where their relationship with the institutions designed for their learning becomes so ruptured.

Clear-cut distinctions among acceptable or unacceptable individuals or acts were once much easier to make. Individuals who did not fit in at school could be dismissed as different, bizarre, idiosyncratic, or pathological; they were, practically speaking, beyond the treatment they would need to succeed in school. Their flaws were seen as individual ones, rooted in inalterable race, class, cultural, or mental variables. Deviants were different in clear-cut, at least slightly abhorrent ways. "They" did not measure up to the standards of the "in crowd." Indeed, exceptions to stereotypes based on such distinctions were allowed only for the few from outsider groups who became extremely committed to adopting insider ways.[48]

We have selected the term "marginal" in order to move away from the negative and divisive connotations connected with "deviance" and with most other labels used to describe young people who have difficult relations with school. Rather than providing a means to separate individuals and acts neatly into two categories—deviant and normal—the shift in word choice highlights the fact that the marginality of an act or individual is always relative and changeable, a matter of degree. In fact, the degree of marginality depends not only upon the characteristics of the actor or action, but even more upon the way in which the person or behavior is viewed and treated. As Jerry Simmons has put it, "almost every conceivable dimension of human behavior is considered deviant from the normative perspective of some existing persons and groups."[49] The term "marginal" helps us remember that problematic relationships result from two-sided interactions between an individual and an environment.

There is no single point at which an individual becomes marginal or nonmarginal for once and for all. Indeed, to define criteria by which an individual or act is marginal *per se* is misguided. What is more crucial to understand is the path to becoming marginal and the process of reintegrating an individual with an institution. We have much to learn about appropriately meshing the conditions for learning with an individual. While we may wish at times to refer to marginal learners as individuals whose perceptions and activities have come to conform substantially to deviant images others may have of them, it is important to realize problematic behaviors are not an individual's total personality and behavioral repertoire. Marginal learners can change even deep-seated, unproductive habits; just as constructive adjustments can be made in relatively static educational environments. Such alterations can elicit previously masked personal strengths that may eventually enable the learner to shed negative labels. After all, individuals commonly classified by labels like "low achievers," "drug users," "class cutters," and so on will demonstrate extremely varied levels of commitment to the roles that have placed them on the margins. Such individuals are also likely to undergo considerable change in their behavior over time. The weakness of these labels is that they falsely connote an immutable condition. Instead, in characterizing the relationships of young people with educational environments, our language must clearly connote degree, variation, and circumstance.[50]

"Marginal" describes a contingent, shifting relationship between a learner and a school environment. The term is most usefully viewed as a "sensitizing" concept, heightening critical awareness of hitherto overlooked dimensions of the problems students are having in their learning.[51] It highlights the necessity of reshaping environments to promote constructive behavior. It implies that learners behave in a certain way in part because they have been treated in certain ways. In short, the use of the term "marginal" to explain student learning shifts the perspective from deeply seated problems rooted in individuals to problematic relationships between individuals and school environments. How such relationships can develop is the focus in chapter 3.

NOTES

1. The technical term "marginal" was coined by an anthropologist to describe the dilemma of individuals whose parents belonged to two different tribes. Although involved intimately in the life of both groups, these "marginal men" were devalued by group authorities and were visibly uncomfortable in many group settings. See Robert E. Park, "Human Migration and the Marginal Man," *American Journal of Sociology* 33 (May 1928): 892.

2. Ralph W. Tyler, "The Role of the Principal in Promoting Learning" (Discussion paper, Center for Curriculum Studies, School of Education, University of Massachusetts at Amherst, Fall 1986).

3. Benjamin S. Bloom, *Human Characteristics and Student Learning* (New York: McGraw-Hill, 1976).

4. Gary Natriello, "Organizational Evaluation Systems and Student Disengagement in Secondary Schools: Executive Summary" (Washington, D.C.: National Institute of Education, 1982). ED 236066.

5. National Center for Education Statistics, *Bulletin*, May 1983 (Washington D. C.: U. S. Government Printing Office, 1983), p. 5.

6. Ibid.

7. Fred M. Hechinger, "New York Adds New Weapons in the War against Dropping Out," *New York Times*, 9 July 1985, p. C8.

8. Donald Moore, *The Bottom Line: Chicago's Failing Schools and How to Save Them* (Chicago: Designs for Change, 1985).

9. "Study Looks at Dropout Problem in Appalachian States," *The Link*, Newsletter of the Appalachian Educational Laboratory (Charleston, W. V.: Appalachian Educational Laboratory, Fall 1985), p. 12.

10. Alexander Astin, *Minorities in American Higher Education* (San Francisco: Jossey-Bass, 1982).

11. Ernest L. Boyer, *High School: A Report on Secondary Education in America* (New York: Harper and Row, 1983), p. 242.

12. Ibid., p. 239.

13. Susan C. Kaeser, *Citizen's Guide to Children Out of School* (Cleveland: Citizen's Council for Ohio Schools, 1984), p. 34.

14. Ibid., p. 35.

15. Ernest H. Strang, "Remedial Services for Students Who Fail Minimum Competency Tests: Final Report" (Washington, D.C.: U. S. Department of Education, July 1981). ED 210303.

16. Lynn Olson, "'Excellence' Tactics Single Out Weakest, But Offer Little Aid," *Education Week*, 12 June 1985, p. 20.

17. Elizabeth Rose, "Black Children in Crisis, Said Getting Little Help," *Education Week*, 30 October 1985, p. 8.

18. Vernon Loeb, "Philadelphia Moving to Promote Students on Basis of Performance," *Education Week*, 11 April 1984, p. 7.

19. Joseph F. Gastright, "Differences between Passing and Failing Students at Grades Nine and Ten: Do They Predict Student Failure?" (Cincinnati: Evaluation Branch, Cincinnati Public Schools, August 1985).

20. Ruth Strang, *Helping Your Gifted Child* (New York: Dutton, 1960); Gertrude Hildreth, *Introduction to the Gifted* (New York: McGraw-Hill, 1966); Sidney Marland, *Education of the Gifted and Talented*, Report to the Congress of the U. S. by the Commissioner of Education (Washington, D.C.: U. S. Government Printing Office, 1971).

21. Lewis M. Terman, *The Early Mental Traits of Three Hundred Geniuses* (Stanford, Calif.: Stanford University Press, 1926).

22. Jane B. Raph, *Bright Underachievers* (New York: Teachers College Press, 1966).

23. Ken Seeley, "Gifted Adolescents: Potential and Problems," *NASSP Bulletin* 69 (September 1985): 75–78.

24. Harold Howe II and Marian Wright Edelman, *Barriers to Excellence: Our Children at Risk* (Boston: National Coalition of Advocates for Students, 1985), p. 93.

25. Kaeser, *Citizen's Guide to Children Out of School*, pp. 20–23.

26. As summarized in Jefferson County Educational Consortium, "Project Student Concerns: Interim Report" (Louisville, Ky.: University of Kentucky, 1977), pp. 16–26. ED 145066.

27. Children's Defense Fund, *School Suspensions: Are They Helping Children? A Report* (Cambridge, Mass.: Children's Defense Fund, 1975).

28. Shirley B. Neill, *Suspensions and Expulsions: Current Trends in School Policies and Programs* (Arlington, Va.: National School Public Relations Association, 1976). ED 127720.

29. Kaeser, *Citizen's Guide to Children Out of School*, p. 26.

30. Ibid.

31. Sheppard Ranbom, "Black Students More Likely to Be Disciplined, Seattle Study Shows," *Education Week*, 21 March 1984, p. 8.

32. Kaeser, *Citizen's Guide to Children Out of School*, p. 19.

33. Ranbom, "Black Students More Likely to Be Disciplined."

34. Esther L. Campbell et al., "School Discipline: Policies, Procedures and Potential Discrimination: A Study of Disproportionate Representation of Minority Pupils in School Suspension" (Paper presented at the Mid-South Educational Research Association, New Orleans, November 1982). ED 227544.

35. Lawrence P. Rossow, "Administrative Discretion and Student Suspension: A Lion in Waiting," *Journal of Law and Education* 13 (July 1984): 437.

36. *Children Out of School in America* (Washington, D.C.: Children's Defense Fund of the Washington Research Project, 1974). ED 099455.

37. Rossow, "Administrative Discretion and Student Suspension," p. 440.

38. *Student Absenteeism* (Arlington, Va.: Educational Research Service, 1977).

39. Kaeser, *Citizen's Guide to Children Out of School*, p. 7.

40. Lee N. Robins and Kathryn S. Ratcliff, "Long Term Outcomes Associated with School Truancy" (Washington, D.C.: Public Health Service, Department of Health, Education, and Welfare, 1978). ED 152893.

41. Henry S. Lufler, Jr., "Debating with Untested Assumptions: The Need to Understand School Discipline," *Education and Urban Society* II (August 1979): 450–464.

42. Ibid. In particular, truancy, disobedience, impertinence, being unsocial, being unhappy, and obscene acts or talk are issues on which teachers do not agree on the degree to which they are deviant.

43. These stages are described in Vernon E. Johnson, *Intervention: How to Help Someone Who Doesn't Want Help* (Minneapolis: Johnson Institute Book, 1986).

44. Lloyd D. Johnston et al., *Highlights from Drugs and American High School Students, 1975–1983* (Rockville, Md.: National Institute on Drug Abuse, 1984), p. 13.

45. Ibid., pp. 9–17.

46. Ibid., p. 24.

47. Ibid., p. 59.

48. Nathan Caplan and John K. Whitmore, "Report on the Academic Progress of 'Boat People' " (Ann Arbor, Mich.: Institute for Social Resources, University of Michigan, 1985).

49. Jerry L. Simmons, "Public Stereotypes of Deviants," *Social Problems* 13 (Fall 1965): 225.

50. See the discussion of terminology by Edwin W. Schur, *Labelling Deviant Behavior: Its Sociological Implications* (New York: Harper and Row, 1971).

51. Where a definitive concept refers to what is common in a class of objects, establishing benchmarks that clearly identify each individual instance as in or not in the class, a sensitizing concept gives the user a general sense of reference and guidance in approaching a variety of empirical instances. See Herbert Blumer, "What Is Wrong with Social Theory?" in *Symbolic Interactionism*, ed. Herbert Blumer (Englewood Cliffs, N.J.: Prentice-Hall, 1969), pp. 147–148.

3

Becoming Marginal

On the fringes of school there is a shadow population of students whose motivation and achievement are stymied. These are the young people who are not being well served by the American public schools. These are the students who have been forced to the margins. The strained relationship that they develop with the educational environment leads others to view them as deviant individuals, either temporarily on the fringes or perhaps permanently out of the mainstream. The environment for learning ceases to be accessible to these students who are having difficulties. As marginal learners, they fail to achieve full and satisfying involvement in school.

Too often educators identify lack of personal effort and weak academic potential as the reasons that marginality persists and is seldom overcome. In fact, we cannot always attribute the reasons for marginality to the learner. Rather, they often stem from low-quality interaction between the learner and the environment. We think that by looking closely at this interaction it is possible to gain an understanding of why so many learners are becoming marginal.

A modified version of this chapter appears in Henry Trueba, ed., *Success or Failure: Learning and Language Minority Students*. (New York: Newbury House/Harper & Row, 1987).

Further, we believe that this understanding is a necessary beginning for action that will increase learning for all youth, including those who have not been successful in the past. But such inquiry, understanding, and action cannot occur if we continue to assume that the cause of marginality lies only inside the learner. Such an assumption releases the school from the responsibility of creating an educational environment that reaches all students.

In this chapter we describe major sources of conflict that can create marginal relations with the school, we analyze the sequence of events typically leading to marginality, and we identify the levels of intensity of marginal students' behavior. We include case examples to illustrate various sources of and responses to marginality.

Because assumptions about and stereotypes of marginal students are common and often false and because case examples can easily be misinterpreted and inappropriately generalized, we think it prudent to explain the selection and purpose of the case examples in this chapter. These examples are drawn from our direct work with teachers, students, and students' families. We have changed the names but have retained other specific facts for authenticity. We have selected to describe these students and situations to illustrate the events of marginality as they occur for many types of students. It would be an error to look to the cases for examples of the typical marginal pattern for all female ninth graders or all male Hispanic high school seniors. Cases were not selected to be typical of student groups of specific age, gender, race, or ethnic background. Rather, cases were selected to show stages and events in the movement between connection and disconnection with the school environment.

FORCES OF CONFLICT

When educators and parents discover forces that produce conflicts between students and the school setting, they are better able to act to reduce marginality and increase learning. We suggest that four predominant forces generate conflicts between students and the school setting. First, contradictions arise when expectations differ between home and school environments. Second, tensions occur when pressures of the adolescent culture are in conflict with behavior required for success in school. Third, frustrations may be directly related to authority figures and rules in school. Fourth, problems result from characteristics of the individual learner.

Contradictions Between Home and School

Parents, relatives, and siblings—as primary educators—create a sustained and intense family learning environment that influences the young child's development. Later, as school and adolescent cultures interact with the home, family members continue to filter and interpret these outside educational influences, mediating their impact on the older learner through daily actions. Parents retain a controlling role in selecting and orchestrating outside influences for their children. When families turn their considerable interpretive and screening powers to support and extend the social and academic priorities of schools, a compelling force for successful learning is in effect.

However, when a rift develops between the expectations of home and school, the learner is caught in the middle. Young people are trained in the home and in early schooling to seek and build on familiar aspects of their environments. They use established viewpoints and role models as touchstones when venturing into new emotional or conceptual territory. Although a degree of dissonance is important for stimulating problem-solving behavior, too much conflict between the messages from home and the lessons at school can leave the student uncertain over which set of signals to follow. At school, one's very language, appearance, and heredity can be subtly questioned or directly challenged. Styles of self-presentation that are polished and rewarded at home can be ridiculed and denied at school. The cues students have learned at home as signals that adults really want them to stop and listen may not remotely resemble the cues a teacher is using. Parents' perceptions of their child's ability and their aspirations for their child's future may be quite different from the views of the child's teachers. When the racial, cultural, or socioeconomic backgrounds of students and teachers differ, opportunities increase for conflicting expectations between home and school, student and teacher.

The experiences of Ramon when he was selecting colleges for continuing his education illustrate one type of conflict that can result when the home and the school are working at cross purposes. Ramon was an above-average student who at the start of his senior year ranked just below the top third of his class. His parents thought he was underachieving, while his teachers and college counselor thought he was working at his capacity. His parents demanded that Ramon apply to some of the top Ivy League colleges. However, in school he was told that applications to these schools might be a "waste of time." The counselor suggested that he apply to the state university to insure that he would be accepted to a college. Ramon asked his parents to meet with the counselor.

The meeting of Ramon, his parents, the counselor, and a few teachers was a stormy one. The parents seriously questioned whether the school had been doing its job to challenge an intelligent student. The schoolpeople held that the parents were expecting too much of their son. As the discussion heated, claims of racism were countered with claims of parental neglect. When the meeting ended, Ramon felt as if he had been torn apart, yet there was still no clear decision about colleges. Additional meetings eventually led to compromise: Ramon would apply to one prestigious Ivy League college, two quality liberal arts colleges, and the state university.

Now Ramon had his turn. The dinner table became the battlefield, and the classroom became the retreat. Ramon told his parents and his teachers that he would no longer be a "spectator of his own life." Ramon refused to do homework and he seldom participated in class. Deadlines for college applications, which were rapidly approaching, served as a subject of frequent arguments between Ramon and his parents. The uncompleted college applications also seemed to contribute to his lower grades and general dissatisfaction with school. In short, Ramon's senior year was distinctly unproductive.

Through prodding and assistance, Ramon completed the applications. He was accepted at the state university and placed on a waiting list at one of the liberal arts colleges. Eventually he was accepted to a liberal arts college. Fortunately, Ramon's experience on the margin was short-lived. Yet he felt that for a time he had been left alone to make sense out of the differences between the places where he lived and learned.

Pressures from the Adolescent Culture

Uncertain about their changing physical, emotional, and intellectual conditions, adolescents are particularly susceptible to (and sensitive about) external attempts at direction. It is bewildering indeed to blend into one's personal style the possibly conflicting influences of the family, the school, religion, and the youth-oriented media. Adolescents turn primarily to their friends for guidance. In small peer groups, messages from teachers, parents, and rock stars are processed through a filter of group values and standards. Many groups are remarkably stable and develop perspectives that influence their members for years. To a degree, an adolescent's dependency is transferred temporarily from the family to the peer group, producing conditions in which a marvelous intimacy among group members can grow from shared confidences, struggles, and values. The same hothouse atmosphere, however, can permit clearly marginal attitudes and behaviors to flourish behind barriers that adults find hard to penetrate. At the extreme, an entire "adolescent society" can operate within the school,[1] diverting behavior into activities that conflict with school goals, and imposing conditions for recognition and respect that encourage a marginal relation with the school.[2]

One case in which pressures from the adolescent peer group contributed to marginality at school involved Alvin, a thirteen-year-old. The values of Alvin's circle of friends could be described in terms like *toughness, trouble, excitement,* and *autonomy*. The group prized physical size, courage, and fighting skills. Intelligence was gauged not in school terms related to collecting, storing, and recalling information, but in street terms as a means of successfully manipulating circumstances and people. Similarly, verbal skills were honed through ritual insults, flirtations with girls, jokes, and storytelling, not through outside reading, assigned compositions, and class recitation.

When Alvin was first transferred to a different school away from this group of friends, he was distant, fiercely independent, and quick to pick up the expectations and limits in the new setting. As long as he could work on his own projects at his own pace, he made gradual progress. However, when another member of Alvin's old neighborhood group transferred to the same school, Alvin's behavior changed radically. Incidents of outbursts in class, verbal defiance, and fighting escalated. Alvin's teachers lost their trust in him. It was as if he felt obligated to demonstrate to his friends that he still endorsed their values. In the struggle between school and friends, the opportunities provided by the school paled before Alvin's need to reestablish the acceptance of his friends. Alvin wound up in court for assaulting another student, and he withdrew from school, unable to connect.

Conflict with Authority Figures

Incidents of conflict over authority and power are probably unavoidable in high school classrooms.[3] Teachers continually exercise authority in ways that inevitably restrict and channel adolescent behavior. They set grading criteria, assign homework, monitor student attention and attendance, and inform parents of student progress. Conflicts over authority and power can be successfully minimized when students believe the subject matter is important, recognize the teacher's ability to help them learn, contribute to decision making, and sense that they will be treated respectfully as individuals. But marginality develops rapidly when the teacher is not clearly in control, when the teacher is incompetent, or when the teacher's behavior undermines the students' trust, safety, or self-respect.

One student's dispute with her mathematics teacher illustrates this point. Mr. Benthaus had been laid off from the school two years previously because of a reduction in staff, but had returned for the current year to teach Advanced Mathematics to juniors. The textbook for this precalculus course was rigorous, requiring a great deal of elaboration by the teacher. While Mr. Benthaus had studied the subject in college long ago, he had never taught it.

Jackie had an average record in her previous mathematics classes and was taking this course to improve her skills. She did her homework and studied for tests. She was also employed four days a week and was responsible for many chores in her single-parent, working-class home. Attractive, irreverent, and quick witted, Jackie was a social leader in most groups; however, the earnest mathematics majors in this class were "not her type."

From Jackie's point of view, Mr. Benthaus was lax in classroom management and not knowledgeable in his subject. He tolerated but lamented tardiness, was unsuccessful in his effort to eliminate chewing gum and eating candy in class, and was faced with constant off-task talking. Jackie regularly indulged herself in all these pursuits.

During the first quarter Jackie constantly asked questions in class, worked hard, and was proud of the B she earned. In the second quarter she failed a test for lack of study time, but she was surprised and disappointed when she received a D for the quarter. She grew less vocal in class and perceived the teacher's questions about why she was not participating as badgering. She once told him off in class, saying, "Leave me alone; I've got personal problems at home."

Mr. Benthaus had retorted, "Stop feeling sorry for yourself. I've got two jobs plus coaching, and three kids at home. But, I have to be ready to teach you every day." Jackie was convinced, then, that Mr. Benthaus was not being professional and was taking an inappropriately personal tack with her.

One snowy morning just before lunch, Mr. Benthaus was trying to hurry through a complex derivation that he wanted to complete before assigning related homework. When he faltered near the end of class, Jackie muttered, "Come on, bell!," a comment that greatly amused the class and prevented the teacher from completing the derivation. Mr. Benthaus asked Jackie to remain after class and assigned her to detention after school. But the detention was called off due to snow. Mr. Benthaus waited for Jackie the following day, but she did not appear. When challenged, she said, "I'm not going to take your stupid detention." When Mr. Benthaus threatened to call her mother, Jackie retorted, "Try and reach her. She knows all about you, anyway." Then she stormed out. Mr. Benthaus avoided making the phone call, and, after two days, wrote an administrative referral for Jackie's failure to serve a detention.

By talking to each person individually and then together, the administrator engineered a face-saving compromise. But Jackie's grades in mathematics never progressed above a D, and she did not continue with the subject. Here a conflict with authority came between an initially willing but average student and a difficult subject, and thus a marginal status developed.

Characteristics of the Learner

Individual characteristics of learners are a fourth source of possible conflict between students and conditions in schools. We consider that behavior in school results from the interaction between individuals and their surroundings. This means, then, that patterns and qualities of behavior are due in part to a person's distinctive nature. Students' physical and mental activities and attitudes can cause conflicts that lead them to become marginal. Yet in the positive sense, insights gained about the personality of a student can be used to restructure educational settings so that the student can maintain a productive connection with the school. Simultaneously, a plan can be implemented to improve the learner's characteristics. By working in tandem, individuals and schools can mesh so that students do not become alienated from the conditions intended to promote learning.

The experiences of Joan, who has a learning disability, illustrate the conflict that can result from a deficiency in the learner. Joan's experiences during her first year in high school show how a proper link among environment, individual, and learning can resolve a problem in student behavior. Without this productive association, Joan's behavior could have been the beginning of the push to the margins.

In elementary school the gap between Joan's ability and her achievement became increasingly obvious. Teachers perceived her as an underachiever. In high school she was placed in average-ability groups, and the expectations for academic performance were adjusted to her current level of achievement. Although Joan continued to work hard and succeeded at meeting the expectations of average achievement, she became unhappy with school. The challenge was gone and so were friends who were now in the advanced classes. She made new friends and received good grades, but her feeling of failure lingered.

The English teacher discovered that Joan's pace for reading and writing was markedly slow. Further diagnosis revealed that when Joan was asked to read or write within a set period of time, the pace became even slower. The less time available, the slower her performance. It also became clear that Joan had difficulties with tests that were written on the chalkboard. In addition, Joan's oral reading was slow and jerky. Although the symptoms of her underachievement started to show, the cause remained a mystery.

Closer observation led teachers to the conclusion that Joan's mental activities and attitudes might relate to a physical problem with her eyes. As it turned out, an examination of her eyes found that the major reason for her underachievement was her imbalanced eye muscles. When Joan became tense or tired, her eyes would wander out and she could not focus. Words would actually jump from place to place on the page, and lines of words would disappear or melt into other lines. When she began to read or write, the words, in fact the total page, would blur and move up, down, or sideways. The messages to her brain would be jumbled. If she tried to speed up her performance, the difficulty intensified. The imbalanced muscles also made it difficult for Joan to focus her eyes when changing her attention from one location to another. Joan's eye problem, then, was a personal condition that had a negative effect on her performance. She simply needed more time than most students to read or write.

Steps were taken to change Joan's marginal status. She was prescribed proper lenses, and she did exercises at home to strengthen her eye muscles. Teachers made sure that she had sufficient time for taking a test. In some cases, Joan took an oral test to demonstrate her achievement. She received special help in organizing for efficiency, improving study skills, and proofreading. The gap between ability and achievement closed, and she began to again feel successful and satisfied. Joan's eye problem persisted, but the educational setting was adjusted so that she was not relegated to limited learning and social dissatisfaction on the fringes.

The conflicts described above that result from contradictions between home and school, pressures of the adolescent culture, reactions to authority figures and to rules, and characteristics of the individual lead potentially to marginality. By understanding the major forces of conflict, teachers, administrators, parents, and students can better ensure a positive resolution to problems that could be the start of alienation and reduced learning. Unfortunately, too many students who enter into conflict with the school setting run a gauntlet of events that results in marginality.

SEQUENCE OF EVENTS

From our observations of schools and discussions with marginal learners and their parents, we have identified a general sequence of events experienced by students who disconnect from productive life in school.[4] The events are all too familiar to teachers and parents who are working to form a productive bond between students and learning conditions in school. We are not suggesting here that all students who become marginal follow the exact same sequence of activities. Nevertheless, there is a pattern to how students conflict with the learning environment and become marginal to it.

First Deviations. Students break or bend rules, usually in a minor fashion, as a way of obtaining what they want accomplished in school. For example, a student feigns illness to miss a test for which he is unprepared, or "borrows" a book on reserve at the library to complete an assignment at home.

Consequences/Assuming Improvement. When a minor infraction is brought to their attention, administrators and teachers tend to downplay or even ignore the problem. At most, light penalties such as admonishments, make-up work, detentions, or apologies are applied. The assumption is that the student will return to compliance with school norms. Most do.

Repeated Deviations. The student attempts acts similar to the initial deviations, perhaps repeatedly, until caught again.

Consequences/Questioning Likelihood of Improvement. Stronger penalties are applied. Irritation with the student is expressed. The likelihood of improvement is privately or publicly questioned. Sterner warnings are issued. Privileges are withdrawn by parents. Teachers regularly question the student's behavior.

Stalemate. The student seeks support from peers or concerned adults and usually expresses resentment and hostility toward the punishers or perceived controllers. For the short term, the student becomes more careful and avoids trouble. But the opportunity to repeat or extend the problem behavior eventually presents itself and is taken. The student becomes known informally as a troublemaker or a poor student, and is invited by other students with similar status to be an accomplice. Often, wary relations between the school and the individual stabilize in a counterproductive stalemate at this stage. It is still possible for tension either to mount or to dissipate.

Crisis/Formal Stigma. An incident occurs in which the student's problem behavior can be clearly documented as extreme. A crisis is reached. Formal action is taken to stigmatize the difficult student, usually accomplished in a "degradation ceremony."[5] For example, during an angry scene a teacher may shame the pupil in front of the class. An administrator may suspend the student for a period of time so it is obvious to others that punishment has occurred. The shock value of this treatment, and the alarmed or disappointed reactions of parents and guardians, can often help the student to redirect behavior in an effort to shed the stigma.

Trying on the Marginal Role. Sometimes the problem intensifies. Rather than fight the stigma the marginal learner accepts it, seeking support from similarly labeled peers. Simultaneously, the student takes steps to avoid the painful source of his stigma. Avoidance behavior (tardiness, class cutting, leaving school grounds) is common. A few students drop out or transfer. Substance abuse often increases. But many students turn to a teacher or the principal to complain about the way they have been treated (possibly their way of seeking help). Parents may call the school to do the same.

Confirming Experiences. At worst, the school, the family, the peer group, and the individual accept the student's marginal social status within the learning environment. The student adjusts to a new role, striving to fulfill expectations for deviance. Parental and school incentive to help tends to decrease because of repeated rejection and lack of progress. Failing grades or continuing behavior problems become expected and tolerated. Rebellious behavior can be the student's final attempt to draw attention to an extreme position or to punish the people and places that have rejected him or her. These incidents "radicalize" the student, who feels a surge of power from temporary "successes" or hardens his or her attitude from the rejection that results. Expulsion from either home or school may be a culminating event that confirms for the student and others the fact that a serious problem exists.

If actions are taken to compel the student to "fit in," the conflict between the learner and the school will likely mount. Sometimes, as the school responds with increasing severity to deviant behavior, the student becomes less willing to meet demands for compliance. In these cases it is easier for the student to connect with life on the margins, where there is acceptance of the behaviors the school cannot condone. The distance between the learner and the school widens as positions harden. The way to close the gap is unclear, especially if the school focuses on minimum expectations and does not explore ways to create or to extend possibilities for productive connections.

Principals, teachers, and parents often bend over backwards to find ways to short-circuit this sequence of events. Students who are becoming marginal receive a great deal of attention and account for a large proportion of the administrators' and counselors' workloads.[6] These professionals "let go" only after the failure of many attempts to foster improvement. Yet the dynamics of these interactions suggest that successful intervention must be geared to the level of seriousness of the marginal behavior in order to alter the student's path as he or she progresses from minor disconnection to serious alienation.

LEVELS OF SERIOUSNESS

The marginal behavior of students occurs in four levels of increasing intensity: testing, coasting, retreating, and rebelling.

Table 3–1
Becoming Marginal: Levels of Seriousness and Events

Levels of Seriousness	Events
Testing	First deviations Consequences/assuming improvement Repeated deviations
Coasting	Consequences/questioning likelihood of improvement Stalemate
Retreating	Crisis/formal stigma Trying on the marginal role
Rebelling	Confirming experiences

Table 3–1 outlines the links between these levels and the sequence of events involved in becoming marginal. The associations proposed here show the typical match between the events and the severity of disconnection.[7]

As students move from the initial stages of marginality toward more-severe alienation, it becomes more difficult to bring them back into the life of the school. Those who observe a student's behavior at various levels can determine the degree of marginality and the form of intervention necessary to reestablish a constructive relationship between the learner and the educational conditions in the school.

Testing

It is not uncommon for a student to experience temporary disconnection. The desire to do well often prompts students to take a shortcut and then worry about being caught. This is testing behavior, which is the least serious level of temporary marginality but still a cause for concern. Testers desire to accomplish goals valued in the school environment, but they see their path blocked by legitimate means. In response, they test the limits of allowed behavior by stretching the truth, searching for exceptions to justify their approach, or interpreting closely the letter of the law to provide a thin cover for what they have done. Actually, a certain degree of brinkmanship is considered an appropriate way to test limits. For this reason, students who employ parental pressure to have special privileges granted, or who "brownnose" to gain favor can be viewed as negotiating limits to create conditions more favorable to their success.

Testing behavior is more serious when individuals temporarily use illegitimate means, arguing that their end justifies these means. For example, students who cheat for a grade, copy homework, forge a note from home, purchase term papers, or deliberately plagiarize are expressing doubts about their ability to succeed in sanctioned ways. They represent as their own something that is not—this is the first split in adjusted identity, their first indication of a potentially serious conflict between individual and environment. Thus, those who clearly and repeatedly break rather than bend the accepted norms are considered to have a bigger problem. Their action cannot be dismissed as a normal outgrowth of the independence-seeking behavior typical during adolescence. Nor can it be summarily squelched.

Some positive value is placed on testing behavior because it can be creative; in such cases marginal people can actually improve institutions. Yet testing can also be the level where students develop tendencies that become reflected in unethical practices in their later professions. At this level a fine line separates productive from destructive approaches to correcting marginal behavior. Still, the opportunity exists to teach principled action and to encourage testers to practice it.

Coasting

Coasting behavior is adopted by those who do not see school goals as realistically attainable or as meaningful to them, but who elect nonetheless to accept and follow the prescribed means because they are paths of least resistance. These are the students who simply go through the motions with little expectation of success.

They sit for tests, but do not finish them; they regularly appear in class, but do not participate; they go to the teacher for help when forced to, but seldom ask questions.

Coasters maintain a false front of appropriate behavior because the cost of authentic behavior seems prohibitive. Coasting behavior can be superficial or deep. Since their overt behavior is institutionally permitted, their implicit doubting or rejection of school goals is accepted as an internal decision. Usually little intervention occurs to assist in connecting the pupil's real interests with school. Labeled underachieving or alienated, these learners are often treated with a casual indifference or "benign neglect," which confirms their attitude of passive endurance or their sense of the absurdity of the educational enterprise. These are the students who are satisfied with middling grades, especially if comparable to their friends' performance. They annoy their parents because they do not aspire for more, and cannot say what they desire to study or how they intend to be employed. Indeed, because their deeper interests are not expressed and explored, they really do not know what they want for the future.

Many adolescents must work through this reluctance to engage. It takes time to develop confidence in one's competence to accomplish in the "accepted way." Those who look upon themselves as nonconformists shun the skill-oriented, group-regulated school environment that seems to allow only conventional opportunities for connecting surface and depth behavior. Yet these adolescents find the best way to be left alone is to conform by going along to the minimum degree permitted.

Coasters are at a turning point. Prompted by the need to consider college or work plans after high school, they may concentrate and improve in school—these students are the so-called late bloomers. Sometimes, they endure until graduation and perform tolerably. Others invest their attention in outside interests. For them, school is almost a cover they maintain while pursuing their other interests. Finally, some react against their own inauthenticity, embrace as valid the way in which they feel different, then act to change or avoid the circumstances that are thwarting them. Once engaged, these can be thoughtful and penetrating students; if not engaged, they are likely to enter the next level of marginality.

Retreating

Retreating students are reluctant to maintain a charade of acceptable behavior. When they can, they reject not only the school's goals but also the available means for learning. The truant, the selective class cutter, the chronically tardy student, the pupils caught smoking in bathrooms or hanging out behind the stairs— these are the young people who withdraw to the margins of situations they see as increasingly absurd or hopeless. Their perceptions are generally confirmed when parents or school officials stigmatize and punish them without providing avenues for productive participation. They hold fiercely to their peers as their support in a turbulent, threatening environment.

Parents and educators must concern themselves with students in retreat. At this level students are taking on a new public identity and, more dangerous, a new internal one. Gradually, these individuals are reorganizing their personal identities around the behaviors that led them to become marginal. As this reorganization proceeds, the likelihood of permanent marginality grows. These students are taking their marginal position and worth in school to the core of themselves. In doing so they lose sight of the constructive elements of their own past behaviors and achievements: they reinterpret the past in light of their present position on the margins.[8] Thus, the problem of marginality developed in school has a contaminating effect on the student's whole personality.[9] Unfortunately, the student's new public identity causes reactions from others that tend to intensify the internal reorganization. For students in retreat, the way they feel themselves to be different becomes the most important element of their public identity, a kind of "master status" around which all other social expectations revolve.[10] The symbols of this new status and identity, such as clothes, speech, posture, and mannerisms, serve to heighten social visibility and to attract further behavior-confirming treatment by peers and by the school. These symbols of their "difference" are likely to lead to labeling and stigmatizing by the larger school community, a response that tells these students that they are indeed who they think they are. When these students are labeled and stigmatized by the school, they are further cut off from constructive aspects of their past and from positive, potential abilities they may have. In this aggressive, defensive, self-protective, negative cycle, the assertive trappings of marginal status lead to the students being dealt with as if they were and had always been only their current public identities. Thus, this treatment helps individuals to internalize more and more of their public identity as the core of their own personal identity. The conflict between student and school has moved inward and becomes inaccessible to those involved in institutional, as opposed to personal, relationships with the student. It is critical, then, that steps be taken to create a more personalized setting if students in retreat are to learn effectively.

Rebelling

While spontaneous acts of defiance can briefly erupt and quickly subside among discontented adolescents, rebelling as a level of marginality refers to situations in which students not only reject existing goals and means but create opposing goals and means. These sustained or planned efforts to strike back are often expressed in school-directed violence (vandalism), interpersonal violence (assaults), and repeated outbursts in the classroom. Since it involves considerable risk to challenge the school deliberately and flagrantly, rarely do rebelling students act without a small support group of co-conspirators.[11] Acts such as using or selling drugs and alcohol on school property, committing arson or damaging school property, or assaulting teachers and students can usually be understood in the context of rebelling.

Most marginal individuals need group encouragement to overcome their personal fears or feelings of revulsion and guilt as they become involved in these acts. When avenues of participation in conventional activities are subtly or officially closed to marginal learners, subgroups tend to develop their own rigid code and standards of behavior. Group members feel pressured to repeat or extend the antisocial behavior that drew them together on the fringes. The danger is that an individual's behavior, self-view, peer relations, and formal treatment will all contribute to a mutually acknowledged, terribly constrained relationship with the school.[12]

Understanding how and why students become marginal provides teachers, school administrators, and parents with three important starting points for effective action. First, understanding the sources of marginality enables those concerned to select the appropriate focus for working to overcome the problem. Second, by recognizing where students are in the levels of intensity of marginal behavior and in the sequence of events in becoming disconnected, appropriate plans to reduce seriousness can be made. Third, an awareness of the warning signs allows for both prevention and earlier intervention.

Schools are often judged by their ability to respond to deviations of students. In this sense, effectiveness is directly related to the ability of the school to intervene constructively with marginal learners. Schools that best identify sources of conflict and levels of marginality are the ones most likely to intervene appropriately and reduce marginal behavior. That students are in the process of becoming marginal does not imply that they are always going to be locked into an unproductive life. An awareness of what it is like to become marginal is the starting point for those who want to reverse the cycle leading to many students' permanent estrangement from the institution designed for their learning.

NOTES

1. James Coleman, *The Adolescent Society: The Social Life of the Teenager and Its Impact on Education* (New York: Free Press, 1961).

2. For a discussion of the relation of reading failure to peer-group status among Harlem boys, see William Labov, *Language in the Inner City: Studies in the Black English Vernacular* (Philadelphia: University of Pennsylvania Press, 1972), chap. 6.

3. The classic study that clearly analyzed power relations in school is Willard Waller, *The Sociology of Teaching* (New York: John Wiley and Sons, 1932).

4. For an analysis of the sequence of interactions leading to marginality by a sociologist concerned with deviance, see Edwin W. Lemert, *Social Pathology: A Systematic Approach to the Theory of Sociopathic Behavior* (New York: McGraw-Hill, 1951), p.77.

5. Harold Garfinkel, "Conditions of Successful Degradation Ceremonies,"*American Journal of Sociology* 61 (January 1956): 42–424.

6. Paul A. Gulyas, "Improving the Behavior of Habitually Disruptive High School Students"(Unpublished paper, Nova University, 1979). ED 180-075. In Gulyas's study, 80 percent of those detained received detention more than once; 27 percent of those suspended were suspended more than once, accounting for 40

percent of the cumulative days out due to suspension; and about 2 percent of the student body were habitual disrupters, yet they accounted for more than half of the administrative case load.

7. This proposition derives from Robert K. Merton's seminal study of deviance in social systems, "Social Structure and Anomie,"*American Sociological Review* 3 (October 1938): 672–682.

8. Edwin M. Schur, *Labeling Deviant Behavior* (New York: Harper and Row, 1971), pp. 52–56.

9. Erving Goffman, *Stigma: Notes on the Management of Spoiled Identity* (Englewood Cliffs, N. J.: Prentice-Hall, 1963), pp.2–9.

10. Howard S. Becker, *The Outsiders* (New York: Free Press, 1963), pp. 31–35.

11. The "sliding partner" relationship, especially characteristic of youth classified as having behavior disorders, contributes to the difficulty of helping marginal students take responsibility for their actions. Sliding partners encourage or at least passively support deviant behavior, then help each other escape consequences through mutual protection. See Dewey Carducci, *The Caring Classroom* (New York: Kampmann, 1984), pp. 34–38.

12. Schur, *Labeling Deviant Behavior*, pp. 69–71.

4

Conditions That Hinder Improvement

Attempts to make school environments more effective in reaching marginal learners often flounder upon an unexamined paradox: the reforms seek to reconnect individuals by intensifying many of the same conditions that contributed to the learning and behavior problems that need to be resolved. Marginal individuals are expected to change to fit the organization. The implied message is, "If they can't or won't change themselves, they don't belong." Few school staffs consider altering basic organizational tenets to fit the characteristics and needs of their marginal learners. In the end, keeping existing institutional arrangements that are successful with most learners but not with all is the unwritten code of many attempts to reduce marginality.

Educators need to appreciate better the ways that long-standing educational practices and traditions contribute to the difficulties of learners who have been pushed to the margins of schools. Further, they need to realize how much the schools in which they work might be dominated by persistent traits that can resist some attempts to increase the learning of marginal students. Like a personality that lacks the capacity for renewal, some schools have established ways of operating that prevent those inside the institution from fully recognizing the dynamics blocking complete accomplishment of their charge to educate all learners. The purpose of this chapter, then, is to consider crucial conditions in conventional school environments that may hinder improvements necessary to reach and teach marginal learners.

Not all schools have these conditions, nor are all schools led by educators who have attitudes that become part of the problem because they refuse to provide leadership for change. Yet the extent of marginality in American public schools suggests that a needed first step is to analyze each school's environment by looking at the conditions that contribute to marginal students' difficulties. It seems to us that efforts to reform schools so that more students realize their promise will continue to falter unless attention is given to preparing the environment for improvement, making it possible for renewal to succeed. This can be done by removing or at least neutralizing the lingering conditions that hinder or block improvement of learning for all students.

We think eight counterproductive regularities contribute to the difficulties of marginal learners while also making reform difficult. Briefly, they are (1) large-group instruction that leads to uncorrected errors in learning; (2) narrowness of instructional techniques that favor particular learners; (3) inflexibility in school schedules that limits time available for learning and teaching; (4) differential treatment for ability groups that leads to unequal opportunities to learn; (5) misuses of evaluation that reinforce a student's status as a successful or a marginal learner; (6) curriculum development and school governance that do not include teachers and parents; (7) unionism that sets boundaries limiting teacher effort and reform; and (8) insufficient and inequitable funding that restricts the scope of improvement to what can be managed in the current institutional organization.

LARGE-GROUP INSTRUCTION

Benjamin Bloom has argued that one of the most significant elements accounting for individual differences in school learning is the centrality of group instruction in most learning environments.[1] In major industrialized countries where schools dominate the formative years of most young people, students are consistently taught in groups of ten to forty. Under such conditions, some students learn quite well while most others learn less well.[2] Schools in the United States are most commonly organized in groups of twenty-five to thirty-five students placed under the guidance of a single teacher for short periods of time; these groups are exposed to an instructional pattern that is favorable for some students but may be far from favorable for others. As individuals move from one teacher to another each hour, day, term, or year, the errors (and strengths) developed in the students' learning in one setting are compounded with errors (and progress) made in subsequent classrooms. As Bloom points out,

> Group instructional procedures employed with individual students who vary in many characteristics *must* produce variations in the accomplishment of a learning task—both in the level achievement of the task and in the rate at which it is accomplished. Feedback and corrective strategies are necessary if this variation in achievement or rate of learning is to be reduced to any significant extent.[3]

The prevailing practice of large-group instruction produces outstanding students but also makes some students so uncomfortable at school that they drop out or underachieve. For students whose errors in learning go undetected and uncorrected, two outcomes are likely if they continue in large-group instruction. First, what is really a mismatch between a student and an instructional system becomes ineluctably converted into the student's own feeling of inadequacy as a learner, which affects his or her aspirations for further learning. Second, failure to learn well in previous classrooms becomes evident as an increasingly intractable handicap in cognitive development and in correcting deficiencies in information or skills.

In short, administrative efficiency gained by organizing students in large groups for relatively short periods of time saves money for the institution, but is quite costly for many students. Because large-group instruction is such a given, educators can learn from this fact of their environments to rationalize their inability to reach some learners. As a consequence, low achievement and incomplete mastery of necessary academic skills are too often accepted instead of remedied. Thus, large-group instructional methods are likely to create and perpetuate the difficulties of learners who move to the edges of school environments.

NARROWNESS OF INSTRUCTIONAL TECHNIQUES

The instruction favored in large groups involves teaching by telling (the lecture), with textbooks used to provide additional information and demonstrations occasionally employed to illustrate important principles or processes. This instruction is designed so that students acquire organized knowledge. The curriculum is viewed as a static body of knowledge—a lengthy set of topics students need to learn. The successive chapters of the adopted textbook form the road map for teachers, and they feel pressured to cover the subject at a pace that unfortunately meets the needs of only a portion of their large group.

The learner who is successful in this narrow mode of instruction needs to process spoken and written information rapidly and to retrieve it easily from short- and long-term memory. Many (but not all) marginal learners lack these and other basic skills of learning, particularly competence in the use of language (reading, writing, speaking, listening) or in the use of the scientific method (observing, hypothesizing, measuring, calculating, exercising critical judgment).

Anthropologists and cognitive psychologists have made progress in identifying detailed profiles of the cognitive skills required for success in large-group, didactic instructional modes. Among these skills are a preference for being analytical in attention and thinking; a preference for being stimulus- or object-centered rather than self-centered; and the ability to abstract or categorize events, ideas, or people into broad categories, using nonobvious features.[1] The achievers are likely to be systematic, analytical processors of information. They can work independently, that is, they are able to structure and make sense out of assigned tasks, are capable and desirous of working alone, are interested in abstractions, are able to handle visual materials, and are willing to formulate and test hypotheses or to seek support for generalizations.

By contrast, lower achievers tend to be more relational and

intuitive learners; they are one-shot thinkers more easily influenced by others. More often, they need cues and prompts from the environment to solve problems, and they have trouble providing their own structure while completing assignments. They prefer to learn in people-oriented work environments, responding best to responsive teachers who use positive reinforcement techniques. They like projects involving auditory and kinesthetic approaches. They remember and analyze information best when it is placed in a social or personal context.[5]

It is essential to realize that these learner profiles reflect socialized patterns developed by family, community, media, and peer group rather than inherent skills. The cognitive skills of achievers are particularly attuned to the requirements of the narrow learning environment characterized by a didactic mode of instruction. As E. Paul Torrance's experiments reveal, many high achievers in information-processing environments become average achievers in environments that favor group projects and creative problem solving. Many low achievers in the former setting become productive when environmental demands change.[6] Thus both "high" and "low" achievers can and do learn. It is the monolithic nature of the large-group, didactic setting in schools that masks the strengths of some students while enhancing the achievement of others.

Public schools in the United States cannot reach marginal learners unless more emphasis is placed on the development of learning skills needed for analytic information processing. Intellectual skills are best developed through modeling, coaching, and supervised practice, using well-conceived exercises to apply skills to relevant content.[7] This is simply not being done often enough. For example, one researcher of comprehension instruction observed thirty-nine teachers for three consecutive days. These teachers were selected as the best elementary reading and social studies teachers in fourteen school systems. Of the 17,997 minutes observed, the thirty-nine teachers spent a combined total of forty-five minutes (0.25 percent) explicitly teaching strategies to help students understand the meaning of reading passages.[8] By contrast, even though ways to improve comprehension were not taught, 17.7 percent of the teachers' time went to assessing comprehension, mostly via questions requiring recall and inference. Not once in this study did any of the teachers have students return to the text to cite evidence for their answers or to identify words and constructions that signal opinion or cause-and-effect relationships. In the classrooms of this study the strategies for analyzing and understanding reading passages must have seemed mystifying to marginal learners expected to "catch on" to unnamed and unrecognized thinking processes.

The need for more students to develop comprehension and other information-processing skills will be one incentive to expand the kinds of learning environments and instructional practices we provide for young people. Although such skills instruction is manageable in large-group settings,[9] small-group and tutorial formats are more appropriate for intensified skill development with marginal learners. In small-group or tutorial formats, the teacher is "the guide on the side, not the sage on the stage." For example, rather than lecturing about and providing a textbook of grammar and punctuation rules, the teacher coaches by helping the learner go through a sequence of actions and decisions involved in phrasing and in analyzing the anatomy of a sentence. If we are serious about reaching marginal learners, we have to teach reasoning skills. To do so, a different teacher-pupil ratio and a different teacher-pupil relationship must be built into the normal instructional pattern, with a greater emphasis on this ratio and relationship than now exists under the current organization of curriculum and instruction.[10]

INFLEXIBILITY OF SCHOOL SCHEDULES

One reason more-varied instructional techniques are not widespread is that teachers and principals feel hemmed in by their master schedule. Into a set framework of class periods and student groups assigned to teachers must be fit not only instruction but all the other activities required to accomplish the myriad objectives associated with schools. Once a school has been allocated staff and has scheduled students, the die is more or less cast for the year. Any student need must be answered within this framework. Three major consequences of an inflexible schedule limit the opportunity to respond to the emergent needs of marginal learners.

First, although students do not progress at the same pace or learn in the same ways, the schedule is organized as if they do. Each member of a large group is expected to master a certain amount of material in a prescribed class period and school year. Teachers feel pressured to adhere to an inflexible schedule and a standardized graded course of study so that their large group, no matter how varied, will reach a preset level of skill and knowledge in a fixed period of time. In this way, the inflexibility of the class period, the school year, and the curriculum work against the interest of these children who can learn but need more time and varied means of instruction.[11]

Second, the conventional schedule in most schools provides limited and inflexible time for teachers to conduct the professional tasks needed for successfully instructing marginal learners. For example, during a school day secondary school teachers typically have one thirty- to forty-five-minute period, plus class passing time and a short lunch period, to prepare materials, to organize for different groups and subjects, to evaluate or document pupil progress, or simply to reflect and imagine. Normally, no additional out-of-class time during the school day is set aside to meet with students or to interact in planned professional ways with other faculty. Many essential professional activities necessary to reach children having difficulty in learning are coldly relegated by the schedule to the teacher's discretionary personal and family time outside the regular school day. Teachers are expected and exhorted to communicate with parents, grade papers, plan lessons, tutor, attend staff and curriculum meetings—all after school and usually without additional compensation. Elementary school teachers have even less time to complete professional tasks during the school day. The rapid, lockstep, assembly-line pace of the school schedule (particularly at the secondary level) may encourage teachers to develop instructional short cuts and routines geared more to their own convenience and survival than to their students' need for responsive attention.

Third, the school schedule limits opportunities for students' social development, again particularly at the secondary level. Teachers require extraordinarily resilient and expressive personalities to be able to connect meaningfully with large groups of diverse students who come like clockwork for instruction that must be wedged into relatively short time periods. Administrators lack even this limited opportunity to develop informal, personal relations with students, who they usually meet in crisis or ritual situations. A fragmented schedule can cause parents and students to think that many educators do not really care. Group policies determine how students are handled, and exceptions to these policies are possible only after lengthy processes of consulting and information gathering. Placed each year in large and diverse groups that are governed by inflexible policies, many young people have understandable difficulties bonding to the school. Such conditions induce the need to escape into small, intense, and often fiercely conformist peer groups as a sanctuary within institutional life.

In a word, inflexible schedules leave schools "frozen." Teachers become so stuck in existing time and procedural arrangements that their capacity to be flexible, to change and adapt to marginal learners, is severely curtailed. What has developed is a "means mentality." Educators confront challenging ideas for improvement by asking if these ideas can be implemented within the already established way a school functions. When a problem emerges, a new procedure is developed that submerges the issue back into what already exists. In short, the means are treated as if they were the ends to be served.

What is needed amounts to a paradigm shift—from an emphasis on procedures and process to a focus on desired learning in line with the school's mission.[12] Both the roles and the responsibilities of the school staff, as well as the curriculum they impart, are currently linked more directly to the calendar, the schedule, and the clock than they are to the intended outcomes of instruction. Minutes, hours, semesters, and school years define the obligations of teachers and students to one another as an organizational arrangement. Too often constructive conditions for learning and meaningful opportunities for reaching marginal learners go begging. Credit is awarded essentially for time spent on learning, since the work assigned by teachers and the standards used to evaluate minimum outcomes vary so widely across teachers of the same subject. Marginal learners are caught within a time-based schedule that is usually insensitive to their learning needs, is not rigorous about the essentials of what they must master, and is antithetical to the structural arrangements that would be more conducive to improved teaching and to eventual increased learning. For these students it is essential to be clear and focused regarding purposes, standards, and learning outcomes, while being flexible, adaptive, and responsive regarding the means to these ends.[13]

DIFFERENTIAL TREATMENT OF ABILITY GROUPS

Tracking and ability grouping are organizational techniques used within classrooms and across schools supposably to reduce the range of individual differences during instruction. This sorting is intended to ease the complexity of teaching a diversely prepared group of students. These practices developed after the turn of this century as the student population and the diversity within the population increased dramatically. To a considerable extent, these practices are tenaciously supported today by educators and parents who see them as the only realistic means to avoid diluting the quality of instruction for well-prepared, able, and motivated learners.

From the perspective of those on the margins, these well-entrenched practices prevent improvement in two ways. First, tracking shunts marginal learners into classes where they have less access to the curriculum content and the instructional practices needed for academic success. Second, students on the margins of classrooms who are in the low, the middle, or even the high tracks are treated differently by teachers and have essentially unequal opportunities to learn. With less access to knowledge and less opportunity to learn, marginal learners are less likely to correct their learning problems themselves.

Students who are most at risk because of their race, sex, class, language, or handicap are the ones most affected by tracking and ability grouping.[14] Tracking is used more frequently in large, racially and economically diverse school systems, and in schools serving primarily lower-income and minority students.[15] Further, poor and minority students are disproportionately represented in the lowest tracks, while economically advantaged children are overrepresented in higher tracks. In the lowest track there is more misconduct, a larger dropout rate, higher delinquency, and lower self-esteem.[16]

In *A Place Called School*, John Goodlad and his research team examined what was going on in various tracks to find whether curriculum content, instructional methods, and social relationships differed from track to track. He termed his findings "the most significant and, perhaps, controversial" of his entire report.[17] The curriculum in high-track classes showed a significantly greater orientation to college-preparatory topics. In the high tracks more time was devoted to instruction in class and more time was assigned for learning at home. More time was spent instructing, practicing, and assessing cognitive skills in these classes. In high tracks, teachers promoted independent and autonomous learning behavior more, related more positively with students, expressed their expectations more clearly, and were perceived as more enthusiastic by students.

In lower tracks the curriculum placed a greater emphasis on utilitarian life skills. Teachers devoted a much larger share of instructional time to rote learning and the application of skills. A more conforming, passive type of classroom behavior was promoted. Teacher-student relationships were more frequently negative, with more time spent on discipline and less concern expressed for students' problems. Not surprisingly, classes in the middle tracks fell consistently between the high group and the low group on these aspects of curriculum and instruction. On most aspects, middle-track groups were closer to the high-track groups in their containing more favorable conditions for learning.[18]

The findings from this extensive study of the effects of tracking demonstrate the instructional advantage of working in the high track. Students with lower achievement and slighter skills, although presumably more in need of enriched curriculum and instruction, are less likely to receive the most effective forms of instruction.

One should not conclude, however, that the key to success is placement in the top track. An academic split parallel to that between high and low tracks is also apparent within classrooms at each track. This split is based on differences in treatment for those pupils from whom teachers expect high or low academic achievement. Research about teacher expectations has produced consistent indications that teachers clearly vary their behavior with marginal learners for whom they hold lower expectations for success. These studies show a tendency for teachers to be generally rewarding and encouraging in dealing with students for whom they have high expectations, and more critical and impatient with those for whom they have low expectations. Jere Brophy and Thomas Good summarize this line of research:

> Both in general class activities and in reading groups, the teachers were more likely to stay with a high expectation student after he failed to answer an initial question. They would extend the interaction with those students by repeating the question, giving a clue, or asking another question. In contrast, they were much less likely to stay with low expectation students in parallel situations. With those students, they tended to end the interaction by giving the answer or calling on someone else.[19]

Thus, even within classrooms tracked to be more homogeneous, a powerful latent curriculum puts marginal learners in their place. Those most able to respond get more time to answer, more assistance with mistakes, more praise for success. Those least able to respond have to react more quickly, lose their opportunity more quickly, and are more likely to be corrected in a critical rather than in a supportive way. Differential treatment of this sort explains in part how achievement levels can differ dramatically even among advantaged children in the top track.

At first glance, tracking and ability grouping might seem to be reasonable strategies to match instruction and resources effectively to students' needs. These organizational means do not usually fulfill a positive purpose, and they persist in debased forms that direct the best resources and instruction away from those whose great need is based on their previous poor performance. Appropriate grouping would establish relatively fluid learning groups that are targeted to specific academic and personal needs and are changed regularly as students progress. This approach demands a much more sophisticated approach to curriculum and instruction than is characteristic of schools using tracking and ability grouping. In place of large-group instruction based on a common textbook and annual norm-referenced achievement testing, teachers must prepare multiple learning opportunities for a variety of small groups that are adjusted continuously by frequently assessing each individual's learning. From the perspective of the margins, this individual attention is the pressing challenge to curriculum organization posed by the school's mission to educate all learners.

MISUSES OF EVALUATION

School environments have multiple and ongoing ways to evaluate learner performance, ranging from teacher observations and comments, peer reactions, and self-reflection to test scores, grades, and parent-teacher conferences. Data from these sources combine to clarify each individual's progress as a learner. If the results of evaluation are generally negative and achievement is viewed as inadequate by self or others, the marginal learner is likely to develop a negative view about school and school learning that generalizes to the entire institution. Thus, students' responses to learning environments depend, in part, upon the ways they are judged by the institution.

In subtle ways, the two main evaluation tools used in schools—a report card using a grading scale from A to F and achievement tests—presume and rationalize differential student performance. The grading scale originated during a time when a tool was needed to signal to some families that their children were not fitting into the learning environment and probably would do better outside school. The grades say it is the student who is failing. The burden is on the individual to shape up, not on the institution to reshape its opportunities for learning to permit success.

Often the A-to-F grading scale assumes a normal curve distribution of learning. Grades are "curved" regardless of whether students have mastered the skills or content; thus roughly equal but relatively small percentages of students receive outstanding (A) or failing (F) grades, and most students fit into the average (C), above average (B), or below average (D) classifications. Applied in this way, grades are only loosely tied to a desired standard or a criterion of performance indicating mastery. What results is a sliding scale of learning, which is adjusted by teachers to rank students relative to one another after a certain period of time has passed. Whether a student has mastered a skill adequately or not, he or she could be ranked A or F depending on how quickly or well others have learned. For students who need more time or different opportunities to learn, such a grading scale virtually assures poor grades.

Similarly, norm-referenced achievement tests label the lowest quartile of students as below average and separate out those with the highest test results. Low or high test scores rationalize educators' decisions to place students in tracks and ability groups. Test scores are used to "explain" poor or superior performance and to support low or high expectations. Again, reference for these judgments and explanations is made not to a criterion of performance indicating desirable mastery but to the average performance of the population, which is the test norm. In this sense, both the grading scale and the achievement test tend to communicate summative, ranking judgments. They are delivered to families in formal, final form, considerably after the time when it would be most possible to remedy the learning problems that poor grades or low scores might reveal.

Necessarily, young people judged negatively by the school begin to develop perceptions and habits designed to reduce the amounts of pain the institution can give them. Research on conceptual systems suggests that marginal learners seek to minimize in four main ways the impact of judgments they perceive as threatening to their self-esteem.[20] The first maneuver is to restructure the perception of an event to make it less threatening. Students who ignore or fail to perceive problems, who distort the meaning of events, or who deny personal responsibility by faulting school personnel are using neutralizing tactics. In a second maneuver an individual's strong points are asserted to contradict the ways critical feedback is undermining his or her self-esteem. Students who claim positive values (like peer-group loyalty) to defend their actions, who reject and criticize the traits of successful learners, or who continually play on their own strengths are bolstering themselves. Third, marginal learners often act directly to remove the refuting edge of an environmental event by abruptly leaving the classroom, by losing homework they do not know how to complete, or by bonding in supportive peer groups. Fourth, some marginal learners internalize evaluation by revising their own views in either surface or depth ways. These are students who submit meekly to authority (although at heart they strongly disagree), who lie or dissemble, or who actively take on and act out the role (fool, clown, troublemaker) that gets them attention in school.

The point is simply that messages from conventional evaluation methods influence the behavior of marginal learners in frequently disfunctional ways that compound the problem. Educators and schools who work narrowly within the framework of these evaluation methods may find that their success is limited with marginal learners. Instead of evaluation tools that use broad comparative scores to grade and rank students long after instruction, alternative tools are needed for periodic evaluation during instruction so as to report to individuals the skills mastered and those unattained in a way that guides further instruction and learning.

Formative evaluation techniques are based on a belief that all students can learn and that it is the role of the teacher and the school to adjust and create conditions where each learner can achieve mastery. After initial instruction, formative evaluation provides teachers and students with data about what has been accomplished and what still needs to be learned. The group then enters into a phase of enrichment and reteaching before summative, end-of-unit testing. Thus, formative methods inform instruction with evidence about what is effective and what is not working. These methods tie evaluation closer to curriculum and teaching that are shaped for the current needs of students.

TOP-DOWN CURRICULUM DEVELOPMENT AND SCHOOL GOVERNANCE

Schools have been characterized as having "tightly coupled" or "loosely coupled" decision-making systems.[21] Tightly coupled systems—like a railroad train of cars joined firmly together—move in unison with clear direction from the leader: the board of education sets policies, the administrators define procedures, the teachers act in defined ways. In loosely coupled systems, administrators in schools and teachers in classrooms tend to act more as independent agents, bound loosely by common goals and general guidelines. External directives may get lip service or be ignored, even to the point where parts become uncoupled, moving off in their own direction. Tightly coupled systems are based on policy, control, and monitoring; loosely coupled systems are based on ideas, interaction, and shared professional responsibility. In these incompletely resolved, dual circumstances, educators become a bit schizophrenic about decisions made outside the system, uncertain whether to treat a new directive as serious and skittish over consequences and monitoring.

Most major initiatives to improve the curriculum for marginal learners simplistically assume that schools are tightly coupled systems. For example, the board of education might adopt a new curriculum package or a new instructional technique that was developed by people who are remote from and are without real data about specific learners. Furthermore, the external decision is intended to be overriding, imposed upon, or added to what exists.

In many schools and districts, survival means continual adjustment to external decisions. While some decisions fit, others are completely out of joint with what educators who are close to students see as necessary for promoting learning. Does one do more of what is externally required and less of what is needed? To comply with a new mandate that seems counterproductive is to accept being incorporated into a structure that reduces one's effectiveness. To resist incongruent required behavior is to be alienated from school officials and resources that are supposed to support learning. It is this tension that immobilizes some schools so that changes to reach marginal learners effectively do not occur.

Top-down, tightly coupled decision-making systems often are based on a need to control limited resources strictly and on an anxiety about sharing power with others viewed as less responsible and knowledgeable. These control systems can create apathy, alienation, and withdrawal on the one hand, and confrontation, power struggles, and controversy on the other hand. These reactions themselves reinforce the perceived need to maintain a system that extends only limited decision-making power to teachers, students, and parents.

Students and parents may see themselves as victims of externally imposed rules and regulations, rather than as democratic actors within a school community or as committed participants in the processes of learning and governance. Like the educators who complain of being locked out of the power structure, they feel excluded from decision making, without avenues for expressing or contributing ideas.[22] Such feelings of powerlessness hinder school improvement and block success in teaching students on the margins.

Schools can concentrate more on learning if those closest to the learner—principals, teachers, parents, and peers—make more constructive decisions about the nature of learning environments. The people with the most data about students' needs, interests, and learning styles have to join in decisions to make adjustments to the educational setting so that students who currently are not well served will eventually realize their potential. It is not a simplistic, either-or choice between tightly and loosely coupled systems. However, there is a serious need to address the imbalance between these two systems. Much more attention to ideas underlying improvement, much more sustained, time-consuming dialogue among the actors, and much more effort at consensus building are required to make schools proactive and self-renewing.

UNIONISM THAT SETS BOUNDARIES FOR TEACHERS' EFFORTS

As a political wedge that was intended to counter hierarchical decision making and sometimes arbitrary administrative abuses of power, teachers' unions grew in size and influence during the 1970s and 1980s. Faced with a loss in purchasing power as school boards held down wages to keep pace with uncontrollable rises in energy costs and inflation, teachers banded together for economic leverage and control over working conditions. This drive to increase the economic status of teachers is a potentially constructive movement for improvement to the degree that it frees teachers to become more effective with learners. However, the concern for greater union control over working conditions must not become the all too prevalent extremist tendency whereby demands of teachers take precedence over needs of learners. As Albert Shanker notes, a "second revolution" for professionalism among teachers is needed.[23] Professionalism in this stage of the movement needs to be based again on service to students.

In effect, teachers' unions have often contributed to the development of a self-serving tendency that threatens to undermine previous commitments to teaching as a profession that provides a service to others. Viewing teaching as a job rather than a vocation has given rise to an unfortunate goal displacement, in which the educational system is conceived primarily as an employment system for union members. The learner is lost from sight when the school board and the union reach a stalemate in contract disputes and expensive grievances over issues such as job security, seniority-based guidelines for transfer, salary and benefits, staff attendance, evaluation of teachers, restrictions on extra duties, and after-school meetings. At a time when close cooperation among educators and families is essential to increase student learning, the focus can shift from the learner to the autonomy and benefits of the professional employee. The emphasis is too often placed on what teachers will and will not do, rather than on what learners need.

In formal and informal ways, unions can set boundaries for what teacher effort is permitted. Strikes, slow downs, and "chalk-dust-fever" work stoppages are three power tactics that have achieved the more limited role for teachers that is seen as progress. Yet the same limits may hinder the needed expansion of the teachers' role to help learners who have become disconnected from school. Professional respect and leadership flows to the competent teacher who is skilled at helping students learn. There is an enduring, perhaps growing, backlash of resentment by parents and members of the community against the union teacher, who is not viewed as one primarily committed to student learning. It remains to be seen whether reconstruction of the school and reduction of marginality will occur within, or in spite of, the self-imposed limits fostered by many teachers' unions.

INSUFFICIENT AND INEQUITABLE FUNDING

While abundant resources and educational quality are not necessarily linked, our society is naive to expect that long-lasting, qualitative educational improvements can be made without adequate financial investment. Lack of sufficient funds is one fundamental

reason that promising ideas are not developed and developed ideas
are not implemented in lasting ways within schools.

When a multinational corporation has serious quality and
production problems with its primary product line, the corporation
spares no expense in relieving its top experts of their other duties so
that they can work with open budgets and experimental projects to
restore quality and smooth production. New state-of-the-art plants
are soon built for retrained work forces. While our society acknowl-
edges that increasing numbers of students do not receive a quality
education, paradoxically we withdraw resources from public
schools. We turn to the leadership of middle-level managers, who
are preoccupied full time with making the currently ineffective
model run. Concurrently, we expect principals to lead in the
improvement of aged plants and of teachers, many of whom were
trained decades ago. The low level of school funding makes educators and concerned citizens question whether we really want
schools to improve.

Public support for public education is fickle, an affair of rhetoric more than of substance. Nationally, although 90 percent of
American children attend public schools, only 27 percent of adult
Americans have children in the public schools. In other words,
nearly three-quarters of potential taxpayers have no direct stake in
the quality of education.[24] This trend toward an older America is
partly responsible for an erosion of political support for schools.
"Tax revolts" and the incessant media criticism of schools are
further examples of the weak backing of public schools. Recent
federal budget cuts are another manifestation of diminished support. Weaker public support and reduced funding are precondi-
tions for retrenchment, not improvement. When resources are
insufficient, proposals for change are likely to be approved only if
what is advanced can be accomplished within the existing organization, which is one that does not serve all students well.

A root economic cause of marginality is the practice of basing
school funding on the property tax. Inequity is unavoidable when
the property value behind each child in some districts is so much
greater than in others. Within states, the difference in resources
available for education is dramatic. For example, in Texas the top
one hundred districts spend an average of $5,500 per child, while

the bottom one hundred districts spend an average of $1,800. In Kentucky the state School Boards Association estimates that there is as much as a $30,000 differential between classrooms in rich and poor districts. There are similar differentials across other states. In 1982, for example, New York spent $2,769 per pupil on average, while the comparable figure for Mississippi was $1,685.[25] Such disparities lead to marginality on a societal level by creating geographic and economic zones where conditions for learning may become less than favorable.

In short, public schools in the United States are resistant to change in part because most of them cannot afford it. In general, schools are underfunded, and certain school districts suffer because they are inequitably funded relative to others. It is troubling that so many recent national reports on education contemplate significant changes in schools without addressing the underlying economic sources of marginality.

REDUCING MARGINALITY IN SCHOOL ENVIRONMENTS

As currently organized, schooling works in fundamental ways against marginal learners and thus makes school reform problematic. In our view, many of the very organizational conditions that push students to the periphery also restrain reform because their pervasiveness and entrenchment make it difficult for concerned educators to conceptualize and implement needed improvements. We conclude that the current organization of the school environment must be acknowledged as one major (but not the only) cause of marginality. A serious analysis of the limits of reform also leads to the conclusion that schools must be renewed if we are to pursue further the democratic mission to educate all learners.

We see the attempts to remove or neutralize the organizational obstacles for marginal learners as a preferred long-range strategy to improve schools for all learners. The accomplishments of our public educational system are respected internationally, and the means for those accomplishments must not be tinkered with lightly. Nevertheless, the reality of marginality demands concerted action for improvement. Clear directions for reducing marginality consist

Table 4–1
Conditions Hindering and Facilitating Renewal and the Reduction of Marginality

Hindering Conditions	Facilitating Conditions
Large-group, didactic instruction	Small-group, individualized instruction
Content-coverage emphasis— learning facts	Process emphasis—learning strategies to process information
Time-based credit emphasis— inflexible schedules	Outcomes-based credit emphasis— flexible schedules
Differential curriculum and tracking	Common curriculum and temporary groupings
Norm-referenced, summative evaluation	Criterion-referenced, formative evaluation
Centralized decision making at the system level	Collaborative decision making at the local school level
Emphasis on conditions for teaching	Emphasis on conditions for learning
Insufficient and inequitable funding	Expanded resources for research and development

of ideas and techniques that are by no means new. Table 4–1 outlines these directions. It is important to realize that the two columns in this table do not represent an either-or situation where the left side is undesirable and the right side is utopian. Instead, the left side represents some of the regularities that, when rigidly emphasized, make school renewal difficult. The right side represents conditions that are likely to facilitate reform and to make it possible for educators to assist marginal learners.

In brief, public schools in the United States generally rely upon a relatively monolithic model for schooling that becomes increasingly apparent at the secondary level. With large groups scheduled on a set timetable according to age (grade level) and subject matter, teachers emphasize the coverage of a loosely defined body of factual information that they impart in a didactic manner.

Students receive credit and are promoted according to the time they spend on learning course content rather than on their mastery of specific content. Students are evaluated more on the material they cover than on their skills. From the results of summative evaluation techniques that assume a normally curved distribution of achievement, students are assigned to a limited number of tracks and ability groups with differing curriculum content, instructional emphases, and vocational ends.

Often the impetus for adjustments to this organization of schooling comes from sources outside the school, such as government agencies, universities, publishing corporations, and special interest groups. Further, most school districts claim that they do not have enough money to make many adjustments. Many teachers and administrators who work under these conditions have adopted political forms of accommodation aimed at improving working conditions and furthering individual careers. The tradition of teaching and school leadership as vocations to foster the growth and development of learners seems to be waning, as does the commitment to an institutional mission to educate all learners.

Any relatively monolithic model of teaching and school organization presupposes a particular type of learner who is favored by this environment. To reach more learners, particularly those not well served by existing settings, requires expanding the school environment to contain multiple means for accomplishing common objectives. Thus, school renewal implies moving in the direction of a school environment that makes alternate means for learning available to pupils and creates conditions responsive to individual learners' needs.

To build a curriculum that includes all learners, we need to look first at learners' academic and personal needs in relation to desired outcomes, not look again to only the traditional disciplines taught in college. Greater concern must be given to helping students develop and demonstrate thinking skills and problem-solving capabilities, moving beyond the current emphasis on exposing students to certain bodies of knowledge for specified lengths of time. In this different direction the requirements of the curriculum are directly tied to student learning, and school subjects are restructured to reflect mastery of desired outcomes.

Further, variable time periods and flexible grouping would be used to accommodate several modes of instruction. To make this workable, smaller administrative units (like the house structure within a large school) would be necessary. In these units, teams of faculty, administrators, counselors, and students would work away from the time-based factory model toward the outcomes-based community-of-learners model necessary for the success of students on the margins. Curriculum and governance decisions would be made collaboratively within these communities. Frequent formative evaluation of students' progress would provide information to guide these decisions. This testing of individuals would be a way to check if each learner is being appropriately challenged. To make informed decisions about the proper match between curriculum and student, more teacher time must be created, along with resources to implement the strategies that are developed. In our view, these are some of the necessary conditions for an educational organization that is serious about reaching all learners.

This chapter, then, draws attention to ways standard operating procedures in schools might hinder progress toward reaching learners on the margins. Renewal is crucial because marginal learners are a product of how typical schools now function, not an accident or mistake resulting from organizational breakdowns. Marginal learners are always with us because (1) we rely so much on large-group instruction without corrective measures, (2) we use only a narrow range of instruction, (3) we accept inflexible time schedules, (4) we track students into positions with unequal opportunities to learn, (5) we evaluate learning mostly after the fact in ways that imply that some students are winners and others are losers, (6) curriculum decisions are imposed from without, (7) our schools are rife with power struggles between teachers, parents, and administrators, and (8) we fund the educational enterprise inequitably and insufficiently. For schools to renew in line with their mission to educate all learners, we must move away from this prevailing paradigm of school organization toward a school environment designed to reach all learners through revised roles and responsibilities for teachers, principals, and parents.

NOTES

1. Benjamin S. Bloom, *Human Characteristics and School Learning* (New York: McGraw-Hill, 1976).

2. Robert L. Thorndike, *Reading Comprehension Education in Fifteen Countries: International Studies in Evaluation* (New York: John Wiley and Sons, 1973).

3. Bloom, *Human Characteristics and School Learning*, p. 29.

4. Barbara J. Shade, "Cognitive Strategies as Determiners of School Achievement," *Psychology in the Schools* 20 (October 1983): 488. See also, Rosalie A. Cohen, "Conceptual Styles, Cultural Conflict, and Nonverbal Tests of Intelligence," *American Anthropologist* 71 (October 1969): 828–856.

5. Herman A. Witkin, *Cognitive Styles in Personal and Cultural Adaptation* (Hartford, Conn.: Clark University Press, 1978).

6. E. Paul Torrance, *Gifted Children in the Classroom* (New York: Macmillan, 1965), p. 21.

7. Barry K. Beyer, "Improving Thinking Skills—Practical Approaches," *Phi Delta Kappan* 65 (April 1984): 556–560.

8. Dolores Durkin, "What Classroom Observations Reveal about Reading Comprehension Instruction," *Reading Research Quarterly* 14, no. 4 (1978–79): 481–533.

9. Theodore L. Harris and Eric J. Cooper, eds., *Reading, Thinking And Concept Development: Strategies for the Classroom* (New York: College Entrance Examination Board, 1985).

10. See Mortimer Adler, *The Paideia Proposal: An Educational Manifesto* (New York: Macmillan, 1982), pp. 21–28, for a contrast of the two modes of instruction described here. Adler emphasizes the need for an additional mode of instruction involving Socratic questioning and active participation in the discussion or production of books and other works of art. The discussion seminar or creative production mode leads to an enlarged understanding of ideas and values.

11. Harold Howe II and Marian Wright Edelman, *Barriers to Excellence: Our Children at Risk* (Boston: National Coalition of Advocates for Students, 1985), pp. 38–39.

12. William G. Spady and Gary Marx, *Excellence in Our Schools: Making It Happen* (San Francisco: Far West Laboratory, 1984).

13. For a discussion of experiments with flexible scheduling, see Joan Lipsitz, *Successful Schools for Young Adolescents* (New Brunswick, N.J.: Transaction Books, 1984).

14. Howe and Edelman, *Barriers to Excellence*, p. 42.

15. Caroline Hodes Persell, *Education and Inequality: The Roots and Results of Stratification in American Schools* (New York: Free Press, 1977), pp. 85–96.

16. John I. Goodlad, *A Place Called School: Perspectives for the Future* (New York: McGraw-Hill, 1984), p. 152.

17. Ibid.

18. Ibid., pp. 150–157.

19. Jere Brophy and Thomas Good, "Teachers' Communication of Differential Expectations for Children's Classroom Performance: Some Behavioral Data," Report Series no. 25 (Austin, Texas: Research and Development Center for Teacher Education, University of Texas, September 1969).

20. Oswald Harvey, David Hunt, and Harold Schroder, *Conceptual Systems and Personality Organizations* (New York: John Wiley and Sons, 1961).

21. Terrence E. Deal and Lynn D. Celotti, "How Much Influence Do (and Can) Administrators Have on Classrooms?" *Phi Delta Kappan* 62 (March 1980): 471–473.

22. Howe and Edelman, *Barriers to Excellence*, pp. 61–67.

23. Albert Shanker, "The Making of a Profession," edited transcript of remarks before the Representative Assembly of the New York State United Teachers on April 27, 1985, published by the American Federation of Teachers, Washington, D.C., pp. 5–12.

24. Howe and Edelman, *Barriers to Excellence*, p. 79.

25. Ibid., pp. 74–77.

5

Curriculum as Environments for Learning

Curriculum reform is a powerful means to reduce marginality and increase learning. However, the narrow parameters that educators place on their thinking about school curriculum can hinder their ability to achieve the very goals they profess. By reexamining their views of curriculum, teachers can be aided in establishing effective links with all their students. The responsibility for helping learners find meaning in subject matter, relevance in educational values, and power in intellectual or technical skills is at the heart of the school's mission. The curriculum is a means to these ends, not an end in itself, as proponents of higher educational standards without a reorganized curriculum imply. Particularly for marginal learners, it is useful to view curriculum as a connective medium linking teacher and student. Incomplete learning and inappropriate behavior suggest weak curriculum connections between learner, subject matter, and teacher. To diagnose learning problems correctly and restore connections, an expanded view of curriculum is needed.

In this chapter we establish a context for a broader view of curriculum by introducing five basic definitions of curriculum. Next, we advance a constructive way of thinking about "curriculum as environments for learning" that enables teachers to realize their key role in making decisions about curriculum. We think the conceptual view of curriculum discussed in this chapter is one that can lead to wise decisions for ensuring that schools become more compatible with their students.

DEFINITIONS OF CURRICULUM

The term "curriculum," a Latin derivative, originally referred to a race or a running course. An image is conjured of undertaking a series of laps on a course with prescribed obstacles to be overcome in a set time in order to reach the final goal. The students (runners) start at one point in their learning and reach the second point by following a set course from which they do not deviate. Curriculum, so conceived, should be the quickest, simplest, most organized and efficient means for presenting and receiving knowledge.[1] Such an image has not been lost to contemporary curriculum scholars, including researchers, teachers, and administrators.

One common conception of curriculum that adheres to this image is that of a course of study. The definition of curriculum as a course of study includes clearly defined subjects (laps) that each student must successfully complete within a specified time in order to reach the goal of graduation (with its attendant social rewards). Due to its simplicity and manageability, in the sense of its being so clearly content- or subject-matter oriented, this definition is still attractive to many curriculum theorists and practitioners.[2]

Somewhat less externally determined, though still linked to the race-course principle, is the view of curriculum as a set of intended learnings. This perspective is appealing to curriculum developers who opt for a predetermined framework that provides limits to the experiences but does not dictate all experiences possible within the established borders of the framework.[3]

Still another conception of curriculum defines it as all of the experiences the learner has under the auspices of the school. From this point of view, curriculum includes the known and the unknown conditions that foster experiences. This approach is considered more extreme than the previous two because it includes planned and unplanned conditions.[4] Going even further in inclusiveness is the conception of curriculum as all school and nonschool experiences. This definition expands curriculum to nonschool settings, particularly to the home, the peer group, and the community.[5]

Finally, a fifth view of curriculum turns to what is perceived by the learner. In this view the meaning of curriculum moves away from the external setting and toward the learner's *interpretations* of what has been planned or unplanned; thus the perceptions of the learners make up the curriculum. Whether it is recognized or not, students *are* altering the curriculum as they experience it in ways that may be positive or negative. Not only may learners be redesigning the race course but they may also be perceiving that running is not necessary or that flying is the way to go.[6]

All of these five general meanings of curriculum are possible definitions. Figure 5–1 includes these definitions in a continuum that runs from *externally decided* curriculum to *internally perceived* curriculum.

Externally				*Internally*
Decided				*Perceived*
Curriculum				*Curriculum*
Course of Study	Intended Learning Experiences	All School Experiences	School and Nonschool Experiences	Perceptions of Learners

Figure 5–1
A Continuum of Curriculum Definitions

In schools and classrooms, curriculum means different things to different people. To students curriculum seems to signify homework, tests, and "all those classes." To many teachers it means printed materials, textbooks, goals, objectives, lesson plans, study sheets, and tests. Principals tend to view curriculum as what is covered by teachers in the form of packaged curriculum programs and materials produced by publishing companies or curriculum committees. Parents often consider the number and types of courses offered by the school to be the curriculum.[7]

We do not intend to argue that unless we have one fixed definition there will be little if any progress toward improving the quality of curriculum for marginal students. Rather, our intention is to identify the merit in all five of the approaches by focusing on curriculum as both externally determined and internally perceived. By bringing in the learner's experience of the curriculum, both ends of the continuum are simultaneously involved. For curriculum decisions to be meaningful, we would argue that the entire continuum must be taken into account.

THINKING ABOUT CURRICULUM AS ENVIRONMENTS FOR LEARNING

Briefly, we are suggesting that the curriculum consists of both the external environmental conditions for learning and the students' perceptions of those conditions. Considered in its external aspect, the curriculum is a complex network of physical, social, and intellectual conditions that shape and reinforce the behavior of individuals.[8] For example, within the school setting learners are exposed to a sequence of tasks, a set of learning materials, a variety of teacher and classmate personalities, and a collection of group norms. From this external perspective, the curriculum consists of those things to which the student is exposed. However, the curriculum also consists of individuals' perceptions and interpretations of these environmental stimuli. As Henry Murray suggests, the learner's perceptions of the environment guide his or her behavior.[9] Individuals actively respond to environmental demands and expectations according to the ways they perceive them. Because the individual's perceptions of the learning tasks, materials, personalities, and norms to which they are exposed also serve as determinants of behavior, in our definition curriculum consists not only of the external conditions that either foster or hinder learning but also of the individual's perceptions of these conditions.[10]

Curriculum can be more specifically characterized by three separate yet interrelated dimensions—the expressed, the implied, and the emergent. These dimensions emphasize the way curriculum connections are formed among teachers, instructional resources, and learners. Characterizing curriculum in environmental terms enables one to recognize a curriculum problem when students are having strained relationships with the learning environment. To intervene successfully when a learner is becoming disconnected at school, analysis of curriculum using these dimensions is a useful place to start. Instruction is a complex task because teachers constantly make decisions about each of these dimensions. Improving instruction for marginal students is partly a matter of improving teachers' decision making through greater awareness of these critical curriculum dimensions.

The Expressed Dimension

This dimension of curriculum typically appears as a written statement that expresses intended learning objectives, learning opportunities, a sequence of content, and evaluation procedures. The expressed dimension is the course of study or the syllabus, an acknowledged plan stating what is to be learned and describing how to teach and evaluate. The expressed curriculum often includes subject matter from the academic disciplines. This dimension is the "planned-for" or predetermined part of curriculum.

Many writers imply that declining achievement in American schools is primarily a problem in the expressed curriculum dimension. They blame undemanding textbooks, low expectations for mastery of course content, weak graduation requirements. While this diagnosis has underscored important curriculum weaknesses, the prescriptive call for more-centralized curriculum planning, adherence by all teachers to the graded course of study, and revised graduation requirements partially misses the mark. Curriculum weaknesses in the expressed dimension are not effectively corrected in a top-down manner whereby decisions about textbooks and objectives are made at a great distance from the teacher and learner. Although curriculum decisions made at a district level or a state level can set a context for improvement, curriculum decisions that reconnect learners from the margins should be made at a local level by teachers, counselors, and administrators working closely with students and parents.

The form of teacher decision making in the expressed dimension will be most familiar to curriculum theorists, since it is closest to Ralph Tyler's classical curriculum development process.[11] Building from a platform of shared values, images, and beliefs, curriculum decision makers identify and organize subject matter and desirable environmental conditions, which leads to planned learning opportunities for students. Decision making continues by initiating the collection of perceptual and other evaluation data to determine the effectiveness of the expressed curriculum with learners. When the plan is implemented in the classroom, a changing set of curriculum conditions is created as emphasis shifts to the implied dimension.

The Implied Dimension

This dimension of curriculum consists of covert messages received by learners from the physical, social, and intellectual environment of the school. Similar to "the hidden curriculum," this dimension includes the unstated and unplanned messages conveyed by the rules and traditions embedded as regularities in the life of a school and in its classrooms. Also, the implied dimension refers to unintended learning that results from what is included or omitted in the content that is taught. The conditions of the implied dimension are further spelled out in those actions of students and adults that are only rarely verbalized or explained.

Learners are on the margins of classrooms and schools partly because they are receiving messages indicating to them that they belong there. The physics teacher who plunges forward with the expressed curriculum in vector force analysis despite the obvious fact that many students are struggling with the basic trigonometry needed to solve vector problems sends a perhaps unintentional message that pupils without the appropriate mathematics background do not belong in the class. The teacher who calls only on volunteer students eager to answer may imply to others that it is not really imperative to prepare each day, since passive membership in class is acceptable. When the cheerleaders are all white or students in the front corner of the lunchroom all come from one neighborhood, other students quickly perceive that these programs and locations are informally off limits. Unless these perceptions are recognized and corrective messages are incorporated in an expanded curriculum plan, some students will consistently feel inhibited by the implied curriculum dimension.

Teachers can begin to make decisions about the implied dimension of curriculum when they collect and analyze the perceptions of students. Students' perceptions of curriculum conditions can be an important source of information about the ways the planned environments influence student behavior. By analyzing perceptual data, teachers can determine whether curriculum conditions create situations of congruence or disconnection for learners.

Collecting and assessing perceptual data can help teachers recognize the relationship between each pupil and the curriculum environment. We have in mind here something akin to John Dewey's concept of problem definition, in which the transformation of an indeterminate situation into "a problem" is seen as the first step in inquiry.[12] The decision made after consideration of the implied curriculum dimension is clear-cut, that is, a situation of relative disconnection or relative congruence exists for individuals. This conclusion gives direction to teachers' inquiry into how to constructively respond to learners.

The Emergent Dimension

This dimension of curriculum includes the ongoing alterations, adjustments, and additions that are made in the expressed and implied curriculum in order to ensure harmony between the uniqueness of the individual learner and the character of the curriculum. The emergent dimension serves as a corrective measure to aline the expressed and implied parts of the curriculum with each other and with learners. In other words, teacher decisions about the emergent dimension intervene when there are excessive gaps between learners and the curriculum to reduce chances of disconnection, unnecessary failure, and boredom. For this reason, the needs of the learner for better integration in the learning environment are the major source of data for the emergent dimension.

As we have mentioned from collecting and assessing students' perceptions, educators can judge the association between curriculum and learning. Other evaluation data like those obtained from achievement tests, aptitude tests, interest inventories, or attitude scales can also indirectly suggest disconnection or congruence. The concerns of teachers and parents for achievement or proper conduct also clearly signal the type of relationship a learner has with the school environment. From any source, discovery of a problem or recognition of a desirable condition launches inquiry. The next step is to identify the specific curriculum conditions that are influencing disconnection or fostering congruence between students and the environment for learning.

As teachers learn to understand curriculum conditions, they can take supportive action to reinforce and motivate successful student behavior, or they can begin corrective action to reduce or eliminate possible sources of disconnection between student and curriculum. Perhaps the reluctance some teachers express in accepting responsibility for making decisions about the emergent dimension of the curriculum derives from their uncertainty that new approaches will be more successful and from their anxiety that departure from habitual ways of teaching will bring escalating problems and more work. One of the difficult implications of the three-dimensional model of curriculum is that no one static instructional model will, if implemented, reduce marginality and increase learning. Instead, curriculum and instruction are perennially dynamic circuits, a race that always goes on. Educators, parents, and learners must commit themselves to a cyclic process of improvement.

As Dewey points out, alterations in a learning environment are experimental, especially at first. From exploratory hypotheses, possibly relevant solutions come to mind. Emergent ideas that "pop out" during the determination of factual conditions are, in Dewey's terms,

> anticipated consequences (forecasts) of what will happen when certain operations are executed under and with respect to observed conditions. . . . The more the facts of the case come to light in consequence of being subjected to observation, the clearer and more pertinent become the conceptions of the way the problem constituted by these facts is to be dealt with.[13]

In fact, as a critical consciousness of curriculum conditions develops, the functional fitness of emergent solutions becomes easier for the teacher to assess. After viewing student behavior and considering perceptual and other data, the experienced teacher can make useful forecasts about the effectiveness of possible curriculum approaches. Since decision making along the emergent dimension leads to more-effective curriculum conditions, the process of curriculum reconstruction should be an ongoing series of progressively accurate emergent decisions concerning ways to build a constructive match between all students and the environment for learning.

An expanded way of thinking about curriculum contributes to a foundation for efforts to reach and teach learners on the margins. Viewed from the perspective of students who are not successful, the curriculum challenge is to create more-effective conditions for learning; these conditions cannot be bought in neat packages from the outside but must be built and rebuilt from within a classroom and a school. More than a physical environment, a learning environment is fluid, made of relationships among people, resources, and ideas. Learners who have difficulty relating to an existing setting need environments that reach out to include them, as well as assistance in learning to cope. The conception of curriculum as multidimensional environments for learning provides the core image for a way of thinking needed to assist marginal learners.

School practice and curriculum reform have traditionally been dominated by a one-dimensional emphasis on the expressed curriculum. Higher standards and clarified content can be useful curriculum improvements, but only if conditions for learning are adjusted so that students can make sense of these revisions. Learners on the margins often read a different message from what was intended by such changes. If no persistent effort is made to provide a variety of additional learning opportunities or to shape constructively students' perceptions of their academic experiences, marginal learners are not likely to benefit significantly from a curriculum revised at the expressed level only. For this reason, we advance a way of thinking that emphasizes the necessity of continually adjusting several dimensions of the learning environment so that more-effective conditions for learning are created for each individual. This broader view of curriculum may help reformers extend the partial successes of previous reforms based on one-dimensional views of curriculum.

While a multidimensional approach is likely responsive to the problems of marginality, it is difficult to put into practice. We turn in the next chapter to considerations for the implementation of curriculum improvement through teacher leadership.

NOTES

1. In his article, "What Is Curriculum?" *Curriculum Inquiry* 8 (Spring 1978): 65–72, Kieran Egan traces the meaning of curriculum from Cicero's time to the present.

2. Joseph J. Schwab, "The Concept of the Structure of a Discipline,"*Educational Record* 43 (July 1962): 197–205; Carter V. Good, *Dictionary of Education*, 2d ed. (New York: McGraw-Hill, 1959).

3. David Tanner and Laurel Tanner, *Curriculum Development: Theory Into Practice* (New York: Macmillan, 1975); W. James Popham and Eva I. Baker, *Systematic Instruction* (Englewood Cliffs, N.J.: Prentice-Hall, 1970); John I. Goodlad, *Planning and Organizing for Teaching* (Washington, D.C.: National Education Association, 1963).

4. Ralph W. Tyler, "The Curriculum—Then and Now,"in *Proceedings of the 1956 Invitational Conference on Testing Problems* (Princeton, N.J.: Educational Testing Service, 1957); Hollis I. Caswell and Doak S. Campbell, *Curriculum Development* (New York: American Book Co., 1935).

5. Robert L. Sinclair and Ward J. Ghory, "Curriculum Connections: Combining Environments for Learning," in *Education in School and Nonschool Settings*, ed. Mario D. Fantini and Robert L. Sinclair, Eighty-fourth Yearbook of the National Society for the Study of Education, Part I (Chicago: University of Chicago Press, 1985).

6. Paulo Freire, *Pedagogy of the Oppressed* (New York: Herder and Herder, 1972); Lawrence E. Metcalf and Maurice P. Hunt, "Relevance and the Curriculum," in *Conflicting Conceptions of Curriculum*, ed. Elliot W. Eisner and Elizabeth Vallance (Berkeley, Calif.: McCutchan Publishing Corp., 1974); John S. Mann, "High School Protest and the New Curriculum Worker," in *Approaches in Curriculum*, ed. Ronald T. Hyman (Englewood Cliffs, N.J.: Prentice-Hall, 1973).

7. Perceptions of students, teachers, principals, and parents were gathered by means of informal discussions between the authors and the participants. Care was taken to ensure that various grade levels and different cultures and social classes were represented. Data were collected in different settings, including schools and classrooms, grocery stores, food cooperatives, homes, athletic events, and shopping malls. We simply asked people to tell us what they thought curriculum means. The responses were written down and patterns among various groups were identified. Also, fifty statements describing the meaning of curriculum written by teachers and principals were reviewed to determine patterns. We did not intend to conduct a highly structured and controlled data collection and analysis. Rather, our purpose was simply to gain some insight into how various people viewed the meaning of curriculum.

8. Many writers describe the learning environment as a powerful determinant of pupil behavior. See John Dewey, *Democracy and Education* (London: Macmillan, 1916); Anne Anastasi, "Heredity, Environment, and the Question 'How?'" *Psychological Review* 65, no. 4 (1958): 196–207; Benjamin S. Bloom, *Human Charac-*

teristics and School Learning (New York: McGraw-Hill, 1976); and B. F. Skinner, *Beyond Freedom and Dignity* (New York: Alfred A. Knopf, 1971).

9. Henry Murray, *Explorations in Personality* (New York: Oxford University Press, 1938).

10. For an analysis of which environmental factors have the most direct relationship to school productivity, see Herbert Walberg, "Improving the Productivity of America's Schools," *Educational Leadership* 41 (May 1984): 19–27.

11. Ralph W. Tyler, *Basic Principles of Curriculum and Instruction* (Chicago: University of Chicago Press, 1949).

12. John Dewey, *Logic: The Theory of Inquiry* (New York: Henry Holt and Co., 1938), p. 105.

13. Ibid., p. 109.

6

Classroom Responses to the Marginal Student

When a student is having trouble learning, four optional approaches for solving learning problems are possible at the classroom level: do nothing, teach the student the skills he or she needs to be successful, change the environment, and remove the student. In this chapter we discuss practical, research-based responses to marginal students, and we emphasize the two general approaches that we consider most viable—improving the student's coping skills and changing the environment.[1]

DOING NOTHING

A teacher's delayed response to learning problems can be the grit that makes a student's learning system grind into gear. For certain students it may spark critical thinking and productive inquiry. We question, however, how often this is the actual consequence of a teacher's decision to do nothing. More often, not responding functions as a delaying tactic designed to preserve the status quo in the classroom.

When educators focus on maintaining and defending the classroom environment and do not attend to evidence that learners are having difficulty, they are ignoring incipient signs indicating that they themselves need to make adjustments. When they avoid facing the implications of a student's distress, educators are usually hoping the student's problem will go away before it demands their response. In some cases, teachers with many marginal students have become so defensive about signs from students in trouble that they downplay the significance of these cues by making generalizations that characterize nearly all pupils as complaining, lazy, or unappreciative. If a teacher perceives accurately the persistent signs of student difficulty and dissatisfaction, this should lead him or her to question the instruction and to adjust the environment for learning.

In the case of temporary marginality it may at times be appropriate to do nothing. Essentially, these times are when the educator has continuing reason to believe that the signals of danger or difficulty from the learner are shallow or insincere. For example, many students have learned that complaining and criticizing are effective attention-arousing techniques. Often, and without much effort from the student, adults react to adjust the environment to be more comfortable. Teachers and parents who elect not to respond immediately to signals they read as superficial can challenge the learner to search seriously for independent solutions to initially uncomfortable or seemingly undesirable situations. In many cases this challenge pushes students to alter their behavior, and they quickly find familiar strategies or develop new skills for solving their problems without further intervention from adults. If not, the lack of prompt response forces students to do a better job of defining and communicating the problems they perceive. Of course, some seriously marginal students become immobilized if their signals of difficulty are not responded to. They shut down at the first hint of unfamiliarity or at the recognition of a problem; these students' withdrawal and apathy indicate to the educator that doing nothing will not work for them.

Doing nothing significant when learners are in trouble marks a failure to use the emergent dimension of curriculum.[2] In extreme cases a teacher's ongoing reluctance to change in response to students' needs will skew that teacher's ability to interpret the students' reactions to the curriculum. Students can perceive avoiding action as the teacher's deciding to do more of the same, intensifying the original curriculum. The actual outcome for most students is that their marginality increases. The academic performance of marginal students typically declines until it stabilizes at a minimally acceptable or tolerable level. Except as a temporary response designed to stimulate marginal learners still at the "testing stage,"[3] the do-nothing response should be rejected. It is counterproductive to leave a learner unaided for an extended time in an uncomfortable and frustrating situation.

EMPOWERING STUDENTS FOR SUCCESS

Some students have trouble learning even when a teacher's instructional approach is appropriate and is implemented artfully. Another optional response to these learners is to teach them to cope and succeed by working within prevailing classroom conditions. For every model of instruction there are defined pedagogic techniques and identifiable learning skills. Educators have an obligation to help students become more powerful learners by teaching these skills.

In chapter 4 we alluded to the narrowness of instructional techniques used in most classrooms and drew a profile of the cognitive skills necessary for success in large-group, didactic instructional settings. For example, much of the expressed curriculum in American classrooms emphasizes content that students are expected to comprehend. Yet little direct instruction is provided to help students learn the dazzling array of skills in content comprehension that teachers require them to perform as they prove that they have understood what they have read.[4] Practicing skills that have never been directly taught does not work for those students who do not already bring these skills to class or who cannot develop them autonomously, inductively, and quickly.

We propose that marginal learners generally need coping skills of four types: learning to learn skills, content thinking skills, basic reasoning skills, and communication skills. Of course, as learning environments and instruction vary, so will the specific coping skills needed by different students. In our view it is the teacher's responsibility to teach students the skills they need to be successful learners. The curriculum of grades K through 12 should be organized to this end.

Learning to Learn Skills

As yet, there are no widely agreed-upon taxonomies of coping skills, and various "thinking skills" programs are in experimental development.[5] For our purposes here, learning to learn skills means acquiring strategies to facilitate the conscious control of learning. Three important types of skills contribute to students' learning to learn.[6] First, attention-training activities help students become aware of, increase, and master their own ability to attend persistently to tasks. Most important is to make students aware of the ways they can drift off task, which is a common weakness with marginal learners. Second, goal setting and time management assure that work is planned in manageable ways and progress toward short- or long-term goals is steadily monitored. The whole concept of a planned approach to learning is especially difficult for those marginal learners who lack an internal locus of control and find the school environment not receptive to their learning habits. Third, "power-thinking strategies," which are strategies designed to encourage students to talk through tasks by using positive statements and visual images to guide successful performance, can help students to develop self-confidence in their own learning techniques. Many marginal learners are likely to harbor subconscious negative beliefs about their own learning power.

In short, skills for learning to learn are basic to the formation of positive self-control; these skills are a complex of attitudes and skills that is highly prized but rarely taught in schools. Indeed, most students in the late elementary and middle school years need assistance to develop the learning skills that characterize the approach of successful pupils. For this reason, teachers who provide systematic instruction in skills for learning to learn assist both high-performing students (who can confirm nascent practices while developing more-sophisticated techniques) and low-performing students (who can start to lay the foundation for future academic success).

Instruction in learning to learn also implies a role akin to academic counseling and support. Students learn to learn by internalizing strategies and habits modeled by successful learners who can reflect upon and articulate the paths to their own effectiveness. This is why the offspring of well-educated parents often replicate their parents' academic success. From whatever source, intervention programs emphasizing learning to learn skills help shift the classroom focus from teaching to learning. Students realize it is not enough for the teacher to instruct, and it is not simply weaknesses in instruction that have led to their difficulties. Rather, they must begin to look to the teacher as a role model and guide. Moreover, they must actively experiment with and eventually adopt the strategies that work best for helping them learn.[7] A focus on learning to learn supports a shift in classroom roles: the teacher moves away from being the "fount of knowledge" to assume the roles of guide and arranger of environments; the student moves away from being the passive recorder of information to become the active inquirer searching for understanding.

Content Thinking Skills

Content thinking skills are those strategies that facilitate a student's understanding of subject material.[8] Helping students understand what is read, viewed, or presented is a central goal of instruction. To "understand a subject" really means to know the basic concepts and large organizational patterns of valid information related to an academic subject and to know the strategies for interpreting and using that information as well as the appropriate situations in which to apply these strategies.[9] One reason elementary and secondary curriculum is organized into disciplines is that students require varied, structured learning approaches in order to understand different types of information.

Unproductive instruction often focuses on "post-study" activities. The teacher tells the class what content to prepare: "Read the next chapter and answer the questions at the end and be ready to discuss." This procedure, which has also been called "assumptive teaching," transfers the responsibility to students for selecting the processes to be used with the material. Teachers assume students have mastered the content thinking skills and can make any necessary adjustments in order to learn the material at hand.[10] The teachers expect to work with students after they have studied.

Teachers who still lapse into this approach find it especially maddening when students have not completed their assignment. While there are many effective post-study techniques for processing information (outlining, semantic mapping, rereading for highlighting, note cards), often they are best applied by students who used other techniques to sufficiently comprehend the material in the first place. Exhorting marginal students to study more and prepare better while assuming they already possess the requisite content thinking skills will not be enough.

Recent research calls teachers to integrate the instruction of content and thinking skills in a holistic approach that pays attention to pre-study, during-study, and post-study techniques. The content and the processes of any discipline seem to be best taught simultaneously. Skills specific to comprehending are addressed functionally, at the times when they are needed to understand the subject matter at hand. The person competent in a discipline is seen as consciously bringing to study what he or she already knows about a subject, constantly predicting what the writer will present or argue, carefully confirming these predictions or revising or rejecting them, and, in this process, comprehending.[11] These general skills of directed recall, hypothesis formation, evaluation, and summarization can be taught separately in the early stages of learning or when students exhibit a need to improve some particular point of the process. The more specific strategies useful to achieving in the various disciplines can also be taught. But skills for learning cannot be left to chance, particularly with marginal learners.

To help students understand concepts basic to a discipline and organize complex patterns of information, teachers and curriculum writers need to highlight more carefully these central concepts and connections. When possible, the fundamental concepts should be introduced experientially or through the use of guided imagery. Gradually, students who are encouraged to describe their perceptions of those experiences will develop more-precise linguistic concepts that will approximate formal definitions. Again, it is primarily the sophisticated learner who benefits from the more common deductive approach that starts with definitions and technical vocabulary as a way into subject matter.

Students also need to be introduced to "discourse patterns," which are predictable elements of organization frequently found in a discipline.[12] Once students learn such patterns, they can seek them in reading material and use them to find meaning in extended assignments. For example, with fiction, students need to recognize elements of plot (setting, characterization, conflict, climax, resolution), functions of metaphors and images, techniques of foreshadowing, ways of establishing the author's point of view, and so on.

Prior to the instruction of new content, a teacher seeking to respond to students having difficulty learning must find out what a student already knows. The information, attitudes, cultural background, concepts, experiences, and repertoire of approaches students bring to a subject strongly influence what they will take from it. Teachers who are effective with marginal learners concentrate on preparing them to learn using pre-study activities.

Intervention during study is supported by more-limited research, but it is an emerging focus of empirical study. Most approaches require a teacher to pre-study the material himself or herself and to identify hints or questions to use during the students' study in order to make them realize what they are doing and thus understand the process as well as master the content.[13] The use of adjunct questions seems to work best when students are guided to look for the overall organizational structure of the text and to use it to help them read and recall. The adjunct questions must include questions about the process as well as the content, so that students will learn both. Teachers preselect stopping points to help students observe the process of their emerging understanding. Because intervention during study slows down the process, it cannot be repeatedly used as a stock part of every lesson. Rather, the learning of content thinking skills is a long process that requires careful vertical integration in the curriculum over time.[14]

With consideration of instruction in content thinking skills inevitably comes the question of how to transfer these skills to new subject matter. Recent research[15] suggests that when learning a procedure that is effective in a certain discipline, a student will progress through three stages:

> . . . (1) the *cognitive stage* at which the student can verbalize a process and perform a crude approximation of it; (2) the *associative stage* at which

errors are detected and the procedure is gradually "smoothed out"; and
(3) the *autonomous stage* at which the procedure is refined and eventually
reaches a level of automaticity where it requires little thought or energy
for execution.[16]

Mathematics instructors who must teach an unending series of
discrete operations appreciate especially how much modeling,
guided practice, individual practice, and review even the best
students must undergo before being able to apply new skills to
unfamiliar material. Especially for marginal learners who have
progressed past many content thinking skills in the curriculum
without mastering them, small-group and tutorial opportunities
are needed to provide enough time to break ineffective learning
habits and develop new effective ones through the three stages of
skills learning. A shift from an emphasis on content alone to an
emphasis on both content and process is necessary if we are serious
about countering the low achievement of marginal students.

Basic Reasoning Skills

There are as many versions of basic reasoning skills as there are
models of the deep structure of cognition. Robert Marzano identifies three basic cognitive abilities: storage and retrieval skills,
matching procedures, and executive procedures.[17] Arthur Whimbey's program points to six basic cognitive skills: thing-making,
qualification, classification, structure analysis, operation analysis,
and seeing analogies.[18] J. P. Guilford and Jean Piaget offer other
well-known frameworks.[19]

It is easy to lose one's bearings while trying to discover a basic
model of mental functioning upon which to ground an instructional
program for marginal learners. Many thinking skills compete for an
instructor's attention, and most are also part of broader mental
processes. While studies such as those cited above are important
references, and the task of developing a model of mental functioning in relation to learning is fundamental for the advancement of
education as a discipline, we have found it more immediately
helpful to start from an analysis of reasoning errors made by
marginal learners in a particular school.

Arthur Whimbey and Jack Lockhead's work with pupils who

score extremely low on the Scholastic Aptitude Test and other tests identified twenty-five common reasoning errors. They group these errors in five categories: inaccuracy in reading, inaccuracy in thinking, inactiveness during problem analysis, lack of persever- ance, and failure to think aloud.[20] Many marginal learners are plagued by such reasoning errors, which stem from low confidence, poor habits, and lack of practice or training in systematic problem solving. Marginal learners usually need help to become better at reasoning.

Inductive reasoning and deductive reasoning are widely ac- cepted terms for the kind of skills related to reasoning that are needed for success in most school environments. A comprehensive intervention program for marginal learners may address these issues directly. By inductive reasoning we mean the processes whereby a thinker reaches a conclusion that is somewhat sup- ported, but not necessitated, by the premises and information he or she uses. By deductive reasoning we mean the processes whereby the thinker reaches a conclusion that is necessitated by the pre- mises and the fact pattern. Many instructional developers are working on skills programs related to inductive and deductive reasoning processes and skills.[21] Since packaged curricula best serve as jumping-off and reference points for teachers, the develop- ment of reasoning skills remains one of the largest (and mostly unrecognized) retraining needs for teachers.

Communication Skills

Just as content thinking skills and reasoning skills must be developed through education, communication skills are needed to negotiate school and classroom settings; but these skills are not easily acquired by most children and adolescents. Many commen- tators have noted that middle-class children have an advantage in this regard, since the patterns of communication they typically experience at home are often parallel to those used in school.[22] Many students become marginal because they do not know how to communicate in acceptable ways all they know and feel.

Indeed, many of the developmental concerns of adolescents can be viewed from a communication-skills standpoint. A six-state study involving eight hundred adolescents found that the problems young people consistently wrestle with involve conflicts and tensions in interpersonal relations and related uncertainties over values. The strains of adolescence listed as top concerns—keeping feelings inside, not getting along with one's family, taking things too personally or seriously, feeling guilty, lacking self-confidence, telling lies, and being ill at ease in unfamiliar situations—all have a communication-skills dimension.[23] Since marginal learners generally feel these strains acutely, communications skills are often important coping skills for them to develop and use.

A practical communication-skills framework contains skills related to listening, clarifying, asserting values, and managing conflict. The interrelations among these skills are similar to the hierarchy described by Benjamin Bloom and David Krathwohl in their taxonomy of educational objectives for the affective dimension.[24] As students progress in skills from listening to managing conflict, they internalize a characteristic response to subject matter based on developing values. Communication in this sense is fundamental to learning any content, but particularly so in the case of the humanities. A teacher who stresses communication skills encourages learners to internalize information actively by developing and articulating points of view and personal ways of organizing data. Marginal students may advance their learning and contribute more when they are permitted to work out ideas and positions as part of the process of mastering factual content. A stress on communication skills, however, allows all learners to benefit from attention to a common need.

Teaching coping skills to marginal students is not forcing an adjustment to the status quo. A teacher who provides opportunities to develop coping skills is actually modifying the status quo. The goal is to develop fundamental skills that will empower a learner to take advantage of the resources the institution provides. One of the democratic functions of schools, in John Dewey's view, is to develop citizens capable of reconsidering and reordering society to allow the fuller accomplishment of humane ends.[25] This will occur only in educational environments where teachers, as well as students, accept the responsibility of continually improving the conditions for learning.

When a student is having difficulty relating to the learning environment, a classroom teacher can begin intervention by investigating which of the four general types of coping skills (learning to learn, content thinking, basic reasoning, or communication skills) are most needed. Students and parents can be encouraged to seek individual assistance in these skills from many sources both in and out of school. This type of intervention is particularly appropriate for marginal learners in the "coasting" stage—those who are starting to believe they cannot really be successful in school.[26] A skills-development focus that is success oriented and geared to positive reinforcement can help these pupils step off the path to marginality. Moreover, to prevent learners from moving to the margins in the first place, classroom teachers may incorporate opportunities to learn these basic coping skills into their curriculum and instruction. It is in this sense that marginal learners can be a powerful source of direction for renewing the classroom environment.

REORGANIZING CLASSROOMS

The teacher in the classroom is nested within school, district, and community constraints that may influence the degree of change possible in the individual classroom. At the instructional level, however, the teacher still holds primary responsibility for creating the classroom learning environment. When learners have difficulty relating successfully to classroom conditions for learning, the individual teacher can do much to adjust curriculum and instruction to connect more productively with the characteristics of marginal students. Some of the aspects of a learning environment that can be adjusted to encourage fuller participation and more-successful learning by marginal students include instructional grouping, curriculum organization, curriculum evaluation, teacher expectations, and use of nonschool settings.

Instructional Grouping

Given the diversity of entry skills, learning rates, and motivation among students within any learning group, a teacher intent on reducing marginality must organize to provide consistently personalized instruction to various groups and individuals. One finding of research on effective teaching is that both total-class and small-group approaches are needed for success in teaching basic skills to heterogeneous groups of average and below-average students.[27] Alternating large-group and small-group work seems to characterize many models of effective basic skills instruction. Core objectives in the common curriculum can be introduced, presented, and reviewed in large groups. Because many students will not master the material during initial activities, reteaching in varied small-group formats will be needed. Students who require more time and varied opportunities to master the core objectives can be split into temporary work groups for various activities, while learners who have quickly accomplished the objectives may proceed to related enrichment objectives to be accomplished in study teams. Students who learn at a faster pace may also act as peer tutors.

There are a multitude of formats for accomplishing varied grouping.[28] Group-based "mastery-learning" programs consistently produce gains in achievement, retention, time on task, and attitude toward learning.[29] In Herbert Walberg's review of theories and research on adaptive instruction, both "tutoring" and "cooperative-learning" approaches are considered promising instructional innovations that can adapt the learning environment to students' learning and behavioral styles.[30] The idea of "cooperative team learning" appears prominently in recommendations in both the literature on desegregation and the research on effective schools.[31] Robert Slavin and his colleagues have also adapted the cooperative-learning approach to support individualization of instruction using programmed materials.[32] Further, the "reciprocal-teaching" approach, wherein students gradually assume the role of the teacher in leading reading-group discussions, also is proving an effective means to improve comprehension among marginal learners.[33] Another promising attempt to coordinate direct skills instruction with more-cooperative, small-group processes of inquiry is the "adaptive learning environments model."[34]

Although teachers should note that there are caveats about each approach, these developments point to the feasibility of teaching diverse groups without "sacrificing" some learners who cannot cope with a monolithic environment. Flexible grouping is one means to provide multiple opportunities and formats for learning. Since every model of instruction can favor some learners while it handicaps others, the effective teacher must develop a flexible repertoire of approaches to use in adapting instruction to individual and group differences. Indeed, effective classrooms often integrate direct, teacher-centered skills instruction with student-centered modes of instruction that incorporate both greater student involvement and inquiry learning.[35]

Curriculum Organization

It is not a secret that learning objectives need to be well defined and appropriately sequenced. This provides a basis for checking students' learning regularly and for providing students with feed-back about the progress they are making. It also helps to ensure that students do not start on new material with serious gaps in their prior knowledge and skills. Despite these commonsense reasons for a clear sequence in learning, implementing a vertically integrated curriculum has not proven easy in many schools. Student mobility, teacher isolation, and limited time for professional collaboration work against curriculum organization.

In the 1960s the opening of the secondary school curriculum to elective subjects offering the promise of greater relevance seriously compromised the sequential objectives that had been agreed upon previously (at least in some schools). A legacy from this era is the image of the teacher as a freelance artist whose duty is to share with students his or her enthusiasm for special content. While artistry is necessary at the instructional level, it needs to be demonstrated in tailoring instructional programs to accomplish agreed-upon objectives with specific learners, not in showcasing teachers' talents. Without an agreed-upon set of curriculum objectives for all students, the opportunity for students to gain equal access to knowledge is limited. Students taking the same subject in adjacent classrooms can end up learning greatly diverse material.

Marginal students are likely to benefit when teachers in a school reach clarity and agreement on learning objectives that are important for all students. To do so, teachers must have regular opportunities to meet so that they can create, review, and refine curricula, thus developing ownership of the major objectives and activities they are setting for their students. This emphasis on objectives helps shift the focus from time spent to learning accomplished.

Theoretically, students should not spend extended time on material they already know, nor should they proceed to new material with gaps in essential prerequisite material. Practically, this implies an entire school (in some cases, an entire district or state) gradually moving away from a rigid time-driven course structure wherein a student can receive credit for a course without mastering all the essential objectives. As it is, the decision to fail a student is difficult because the remedial opportunities are limited. Without a clear set of objectives and a variety of means available to accomplish each one, a teacher deciding about failing a student must calculate the benefit of spending extended time on incomplete objectives (in a summer school or repeated course) versus the cost of spending extra time on objectives that have already been mastered. As an interim step, course prerequisites could be set according to objectives mastered, which would free a teacher from having to decide whether to continue with scheduled new material or to focus on preliminary objectives that have not been mastered by unprepared students. Various means to master prerequisite objectives prior to a student's entering a course would also have to be designed if the need emerged.

In the current organization of curriculum, adjustments in the placement of marginal learners can be made by nonpromotion, grade acceleration, and repetition of a course. The consequences of each of these decisions for students' social and intellectual development must be considered carefully. A more refined curriculum organization is needed, one that is based on a sequence of key objectives for all students. Within such a system, teachers need to move away from the instructional paradigm that includes presentation of information to the total class, little explanation of cognitive tasks, use of the same repetitive practice materials by all students, and evaluation emphasizing one correct answer.[36] The curriculum should be organized to emphasize core (and related enrichment or prerequisite) objectives, multiple means for learning each objective according to differing learning styles and resources, temporary grouping during reteaching, and evaluation at various times during the learning. Instruction with these elements is consistent with our view of curriculum as environments for learning, in which intended objectives (the expressed dimension) are internalized in idiosyncratic ways by learners (the implied dimension). Information about what students have learned leads the teacher to make alterations and adjustments in the learning environment that are designed to provide a variety of opportunities aimed at effective means for learning various objectives (the emergent dimension).

Curriculum Evaluation

Crucial to curriculum reorganization is the use of evaluation connected to each objective. In attempting to reach marginal students, evaluation is used to determine the presence of specific competencies and to assess progress through the learning sequence. Evaluation provides information for teachers to use in forming learning groups and in selecting learning opportunities. It is more often geared in a formative way to provide direction for adjusting the learning environment, and it is less often geared in a summative way to determine who passes with a high grade and who fails (often to be left behind with inadequate skills for learning on his or her own).

It is time to move beyond skills testing, as well. In this dawning era of electronic data bases, individual teachers must still be able to develop a system for collecting, recording, and using information about students' strengths, interests, and learning styles. Despite their capability for extraordinary insight into individual learners, most teachers have haphazard, informal systems for collecting and storing the information they need to tailor their curriculum and instruction to particular students or groups. The greater shame is that each teacher basically starts the diagnostic process from scratch with new students, which leaves little opportunity to benefit from the insights of previous and current teachers. The challenge is to build a data base about what students are learning and about how they learn best, and to use these data to make curricular and instructional decisions.

According to a common saying, we should be teaching pupils, not teaching subjects. Evaluation has to give us information about learning as well as about the content learned. For practical purposes, teachers need accessible strategies that connect with the most powerful interests and the best-developed processes their students have for using information. They also need to know what student thinking skills are weak before they can make intelligent decisions about what to bolster. They need to know how students work together—who learns best when they are the oldest or the youngest, the fastest or the slowest, the old buddy or the newcomer in a group.

Perhaps the rationale is clearest for developing such a data base with marginal students first. Probably one of the most rewarding steps teachers can take is to bring together all the teachers, the counselor, and the parents of a student who is not learning well. When frustrations as well as modest successes are discussed, all participants grow more sensitive to the conditions this learner needs to be able to respond constructively. Some schools may form ad hoc staff development teams to increase teachers' skills in dealing with marginal students. For students having difficulty relating to and learning from the existing classroom learning environment, evaluation should help teachers figure out how, and under what conditions, the students learn best, so that through proper curriculum and instruction they can empower the students to strengthen their learning and to increase their responsibility for successful learning.

Teacher Expectations

Teachers treat individual students differently. They may do so out of dislike or bias, or they may do so because they perceive them as differing in academic potential and temperament. When working with marginal students, teachers must examine and possibly alter the ways they communicate differential expectations to each student.

Thomas Good and Rhona Weinstein identified six general dimensions for teachers' communication of differential expectations: task environment, grouping practices, locus of responsibility for learning, feedback and evaluation practices, motivational strategies, and quality of teacher relationships.[37] These dimensions suggest a broad range of ways in which teachers use the learning environment to let various children know what is expected of them. Expectations, in this case, are defined as inferences that teachers make about the future academic achievement of students and about the types of classroom assignments that students need, given their present abilities and potential achievement. Research conducted on expectations has found trends in the ways students are typically treated based on teachers' perceptions of students' ability levels. The following findings are presented as examples related to each dimension for communicating differential expectations. Although not all teachers behave as the findings suggest, the research shows clear tendencies.

Students believed to be more capable have more opportunity to perform publicly on meaningful tasks, while students viewed as less capable have fewer opportunities and are given more low-level tasks (task environment). High-ability groups receive more assignments demanding comprehension and insight, while groups seen as having less ability have little choice in their assignments and are given more drill and practice activities (grouping practices).

Students viewed as more capable have more autonomy and responsibility for decisions about assignments, and they are given more time to work. Less capable students are frequently monitored and regularly interrupted, because the teacher assumes greater responsibility for their progress (locus of responsibility). Students seen as having more ability are more likely than lower-ability children to be encouraged to evaluate their own progress and to be requested to provide their judgments about the effectiveness of teachers (feedback and evaluation). Students seen as less capable receive less honest, less contingent, and more gratuitous or patronizing "pat-on-the-back" feedback, while more-capable students receive more honest progress reports directly related to their performance (motivation). In short, teachers tend to communicate their level of expectation by the degree to which they show respect for students as individuals with unique interests and needs (quality of teacher relationships).[38]

Classrooms are complex environments wherein both teachers and students must often interpret ambiguous behavior. The problem with expectations is not so much that individuals are seen as having different potential and thus are treated differently; rather the subtle and insidious nature of expectations is that students and teachers tend to form an initial impression of the way each regards the other that influences future decisions and actions. These impressions are based on initial events that have taken place in a very specific kind of environment (a classroom), and are not necessarily predictive to the wide range of behaviors a person must develop for successful learning. However, teachers are likely to interpret subsequent student behavior in line with their original perceptions. Since expectations are communicated along at least six general dimensions, it is easy for teacher-student relations to stabilize in a continually reinforced cycle that matches the persistent expectations. Even when a teacher begins to treat a student differently, or when a student begins a new campaign to improve, it takes time for the new behavior to be recognized and supported. Thus, marginal students know only too well (at least in their own minds) where they stand with a teacher. Students who are not succeeding in school tend to be pessimistic about the likelihood of altering their position or performance. Marginal learners need to change the signals they send in order to show teachers their academic talents and true desire to improve, and teachers must alter the multiple ways their behavior may send the steady message that they have low expectations for certain pupils.

Nonschool Settings

In highlighting the need for teachers to alter their thinking toward some learners and to reorganize classrooms for marginal students, we must be careful not to overemphasize the teacher as the central actor in the classroom and the primary "maker" of the student "product" that comes out at the end of the year. Parents, siblings, relatives, religious leaders, coaches, and peers (not to mention radios, telephones, records, televisions, movies, and microcomputers) open up numerous ways of gaining skills and attitudes. Curriculum reform within classrooms alone will not produce hoped-for improvements with marginal students unless constructive adjustments are made in the ways the school curriculum connects with other agencies, individuals, and experiences that educate outside the school.

Teachers may play a central role in making curriculum connections between school and nonschool settings so that marginal and other students can increase their learning. For example, teachers can capitalize on experiences already taking place in the learner's life outside school. One study found that marginal students differed greatest from their classmates in how much interests and problems from outside school interfered with their school work. The home and community responsibilities of marginal students did not permit the same degree of concentration on school work, nor did these less successful students see the school curriculum as equally relevant to their concerns.[39] In an "informal" way teachers must refer to and draw upon outside experiences to make the school curriculum more engaging and effective.

Also, school and nonschool environments can be deliberately combined. In this "formal" approach the teacher supplements classroom learning by organizing opportunities for short-term exposure to people, places, and things from the community. These opportunities permit marginal students and other students to see course content from a variety of realistic perspectives, thus heightening interest and involvement beyond what a textbook can stimulate.

Further, teachers may make arrangements for learning outside school. Students are placed in other settings (work-study, internships, shadowing experiences) for specific experiences for a set time period. This "nonformal"[40] approach creates opportunities for systematic learning that is related to the school curriculum but takes place under the authority of another agency of educational importance. For a student having difficulty learning and connecting with school, such conditions in nonschool experiences sometimes open the student's eyes to the value of the learning and habits emphasized by schools.[41]

Reorganizing the classroom learning environment can be a complex, multidimensional response to learners who are having difficulty. An ongoing effort to adjust learning environments and to improve curriculum and instruction should be a normal part of a self-renewing school. Indeed, in Dewey's terms the basic function of a teacher is to organize and reorganize a learning environment that provides opportunities for students to act, reflect, and grow. It becomes imperative to analyze seriously and to reconstruct in major ways the instructional grouping, curriculum sequence, evaluation procedures, teacher expectations, or use of nonschool settings when learners show signs of "retreating," either internally or physically, from the setting designed for learning. Marginal students in retreat are rejecting the means available for learning and are questioning whether the goals of the school can be meaningful for them.[42] They are often beyond the point of being rescued by their teachers' tinkering with the instructional program or coaching to help them learn how to make the most of the current setting. Unfortunately, the large numbers of students who are not achieving and who drop out, cut class, fail to attend, or retreat into drugs or other unconstructive subcultures are compelling evidence of the need for serious renewal of classrooms that gives all students equal access to quality learning.

REMOVING THE STUDENT

When learning difficulties first become evident, and particularly if a confrontational incident between student and teacher occurs, the first move often proposed by concerned parents and students is to remove the learner from the classroom environment, which they view as ineffective or offending. Teachers often hasten to agree with this approach, demanding removal when they are irritated by a confrontational incident or subtly encouraging removal in conversations with parents and students. The seductive attraction of removing a student is that it eliminates the immediate frustration on all sides. Both family and teacher may wash their hands of a situation without painfully reassessing their own behavior or the conditions that might have contributed to the problem. Too often, removing the student is a quick, political fix that has little to do with increasing the student's learning.

Simply removing a student without detailed analysis of the situation assumes that the receiving environment will be more productive—an assumption that cannot always be sustained because major differences between the two settings are not likely and the patterns of behavior a student brings to the new setting have not changed. Further, if the settings are indeed different in major ways, considerable slippage may occur for the transferring student and the receiving class members as the adjustment period and orientation process take place. Since removing students also removes one incentive for changing a learning environment, we are not likely to find the desired diversity when removing students is a common practice.

Premature removal may deny students opportunities to address their own learning or behavioral weaknesses. Similarly, if the difficulty stems from a weakness of the teacher, removing the student simply covers up the deficiency until it emerges with another pupil. In this sense, the quick fix avoids a close look at the problem. Administrators and teachers should grasp this opportunity to address the weaknesses of teachers and students by constructive consideration of penetrating, unavoidable questions central to the decision for removal.

There are indeed circumstances when removing a student is necessary to avoid the damaging side-effects of a mismatch between the classroom environment and the student's characteristics. One circumstance is when serious physical or emotional damage is likely to result from continuing in a setting. Evidence of this likelihood includes threats of assault or actual assault, confirmation from a consulting professional that a student in trouble is particularly vulnerable to being hurt in a setting, or a rapidly escalating series of intensifying incidents that result in mounting conflict between the student and the teacher. Another circumstance warranting removal is when a protracted, good-faith series of efforts to adjust the learning environment and develop new coping skills results in objective evidence of failure. Still, the teacher, the principal, the parent, and the student need a basis for determining that the transfer will benefit the student because of new opportunities that will be created.

In order to eliminate negative perceptions and counter possible resistance, consideration also needs to be given to the teacher who is going to receive the student. Transferring students with problems from one classroom to another may be viewed by receiving teachers as a "dump job." A sympathetic new lease on classroom life is not always readily available for students who are perceived to be unwilling to alter their own behavior.

Removing a marginal student should be considered as a late

stage in intervention. For example, it should be used with students who are committed to active rebellion, whose rejection of school goals and means includes setting up countering goals that may damage other persons, school property, or themselves. In addition, the severely withdrawn or retreating individual, who simply cannot respond to existing efforts to reach him or her, may well benefit from a change of venue.

In this chapter we have reviewed four optional approaches that can be used at the classroom level to help marginal learners: doing nothing, teaching coping skills, reorganizing classrooms, and removing the student. The classroom teacher working alone can have an impact on reducing marginality, primarily by incorporating coping skills in the curriculum and by carefully adjusting the learning environment to provide favorable conditions for learners. In many cases, however, what the individual teacher can accomplish is not sufficient to reverse the marginal student's low achievement. It also takes coordinated action at the schoolwide level by a team of parents and members of the community acting in concert with the teacher and the principal. Reducing marginality at the school and family levels are thus the topics of the next two chapters.

NOTES

1. For an introduction to the four responses possible when learners are marginal to an instructional model, see Bruce Joyce, "Instructional Models and 'Marginal' Learners" (Paper presented at the Annual Meeting of the American Educational Research Association, Montreal, 1983).

2. See chapter 5 for a discussion of the dynamics of the three curriculum dimensions.

3. See chapter 3 for a description of the four stages of intensity in marginal behavior.

4. Dolores Durkin, "What Classroom Observations Reveal about Reading Comprehension Instruction," *Reading Research Quarterly* 14, no. 4 (1978–79): 481–533.

5. Paul Chance, *Thinking in the Classroom: A Survey of Programs* (New York: Teachers College Press, 1980).

6. Robert J. Marzano and Daisy E. Arredondo, "Restructuring Schools through the Teaching of Thinking Skills," *Educational Leadership* 43 (May 1986): 21.

7. For an analysis of intervention programs to promote skills in learning to learn, see Barbara L. McCombs, "Processes and Skills Underlying Continuing

Intrinsic Motivation to Learn: Toward a Definition of Motivational Skills Training Interventions," *Educational Psychologist* 19 (Fall 1984): 199–218.

8. Marzano and Arredondo, "Restructuring Schools through the Teaching of Thinking Skills," p. 21.

9. Walter Doyle, "Academic Work," *Review of Educational Research* 53 (Summer 1983): 159–199.

10. Olive S. Niles, "Integration of Content and Skills Instruction," in *Reading, Thinking, and Concept Development*, ed. Theodore L. Harris and Eric J. Cooper (New York: College Entrance Examination Board, 1985), p. 179.

11. Ibid., p. 178.

12. Robert Marzano and Janice Dole, *Teaching Basic Relationships and Patterns of Ideas* (Denver: Mid-Continent Regional Education Laboratory, 1985). This book identifies five basic patterns or discourse types in stories and textbooks.

13. Niles, "Integration of Content and Skills Instruction," p. 181.

14. See ibid., pp. 180–190, for a review of research on during-reading activities, along with several examples of adjunct question formats.

15. John R. Anderson, "Acquisition of Cognitive Skills," *Psychological Review* 89 (July 1982): 369–406.

16. Marzano and Arredondo, "Restructuring Schools through the Teaching of Thinking Skills," p. 22.

17. Ibid., p. 23. See also, John R. Anderson, *The Architecture of Cognition* (Cambridge, Mass.: Harvard University Press, 1983), p. 47.

18. Arthur Whimbey, *Strategic Reasoning* (Stamford, Conn.: Innovative Sciences, 1985).

19. J. P. Guilford, *The Nature of Human Intelligence* (New York: McGraw-Hill, 1967); Howard Gruber and J. Jacques Voneche, eds., *The Essential Piaget* (New York: Basic Books, 1977).

20. Arthur Whimbey and Jack Lockhead, *Problem Solving and Comprehension*, 3d ed. (Hillsdale, N.J.: Lawrence Erlbaum Associates, 1985), pp. 11–20.

21. To identify programs to review, see Chance, *Thinking in the Classroom*; Raymond S. Nickerson, "Kinds of Thinking Taught in Current Programs," *Educational Leadership* 42 (September 1984): 26–37; Arthur L. Costa, ed., *Developing Minds: A Resource Book for Teaching Thinking* (Alexandria, Va.: Association for Supervision and Curriculum Development, 1985). See also, Anita Harnadek, *Inferences A and B: Inductive Thinking Skills* (Pacific Grove, Calif.: Midwest Publications Co., 1979); Stephen Toulmin, Richard Rieke, and Allan Janik, *An Introduction to Reasoning* (New York: Macmillan, 1979); and Jonathan Baron, "What Kinds of Intelligence Components Are Fundamental?" in *Thinking and Learning Skills*, vol. 2, *Research and Open Questions*, ed. Susan F. Chipman, Judith W. Segal, and Robert Glaser (Hillsdale, N.J.: Lawrence Erlbaum Associates, 1985).

22. Basil B. Bernstein, *Class, Codes, and Control* (London: Routledge and Kegan Paul, 1971–1975).

23. Quoted in *Guide to "On the Level"* (Bloomington, Ind.: Agency for Instructional Television, 1980), p. 10.

24. David Krathwohl, Benjamin Bloom, and Bertram Masia, *Taxonomy of Educational Objectives: The Affective Domain* (New York: McKay, 1956).

25. John Dewey, *Democracy and Education: An Introduction to the Philosophy of Education* (New York: Free Press, 1916).

26. See chapter 3 for a description of marginal learners at the coasting stage.

27. Jane Stallings, Margaret Needels, and Nancy Stayrook, *How to Change the Process of Teaching Basic Reading Skills in Secondary Schools*, Final Report to the National Institute of Education (Menlo Park, Calif.: SRI International, 1979).

28. An interesting appendix of learning group configurations classified according to instructional purpose and learner role can be found in Jeanne Masson-Douglas, "Learning Environments of Small Rural Schools: A Profile of Selected One-Room Schools in Rural Communities of New England" (Doct. diss., University of Massachusetts at Amherst, 1982).

29. Thomas R. Guskey and Sally L. Gates, "Synthesis of Research on the Effects of Mastery Learning in Elementary and Secondary Classrooms," *Educational Leadership* 43 (May 1986): 73–79.

30. Herbert J. Walberg, "Instructional Theories and Research Evidence," in *Adapting Instruction to Individual Differences*, ed. Margaret C. Wang and Herbert J. Walberg (Berkeley, Calif.: McCutchan Publishing Corp., 1985), pp. 3–23. See also, Peter A. Cohen, James A. Kulik, and Chen-Lin C. Kulik, "Educational Outcomes of Tutoring: A Meta-Analysis of Findings," *American Educational Research Journal* 19 (Summer 1982): 237–248.

31. Bruce R. Hare and Daniel U. Levine, "Effective Schooling in Desegregated Settings: What Do We Know about Learning Style and Linguistic Differences?" *Equity and Choice* 1 (Winter 1985): 13–18.

32. Robert E. Slavin, "Team-Assisted Individualization: A Cooperative Learning Solution for Adaptive Instruction in Mathematics," in *Adapting Instruction to Individual Differences*, ed. Wang and Walberg, pp. 236–253.

33. Annemarie Palincsar and Ann Brown, "Reciprocal Teaching: Activities to Promote 'Reading with Your Mind'," in *Reading, Thinking, and Concept Development*, ed. Harris and Cooper, pp. 147–159.

34. Margaret C. Wang, "Adaptive Instruction: Building on Diversity," *Theory Into Practice* 19 (Spring 1980): 122–127.

35. Hare and Levine, "Effective Schooling in Desegregated Settings," p. 18.

36. This is the most common instructional paradigm for the teaching of reading according to a review of research conducted by P. David Pearson and Robert Tierney, "In Search of a Model of Instructional Research in Reading," in *Learning and Motivation in the Classroom*, ed. Scott G. Paris, Gary M. Olson, and Harold W. Stevenson (Hillsdale, N.J.: Lawrence Erlbaum Associates, 1983).

37. Thomas C. Good and Rhona S. Weinstein, "Teacher Expectations: A Framework for Exploring Classrooms," in *Improving Teaching*, 1986 ASCD Yearbook (Alexandria, Va.: Association for Supervision and Curriculum Development, 1986), pp. 63–85.

38. Ibid., p. 72.

39. Ward J. Ghory, "Alternative Educational Environments: Marginal Learner Perceptions of Curriculum Conditions in Public Alternative High Schools" (Doct. diss., University of Massachusetts at Amherst, 1977), p. 241.

40. Our use of the terms "formal," "informal," and "nonformal" follows the definitions advanced in Philip H. Coombs with Manzoor Ahmed, *Attacking Rural Poverty: How Nonformal Education Can Help*, a research report for the World Bank prepared by the International Council for Educational Development (Baltimore: Johns Hopkins University Press, 1974), pp. 7–9.

41. Robert L. Sinclair and Ward J. Ghory, "Curriculum Connections: Combining Environments for Learning," in *Education in School and Nonschool Settings*, ed. Mario D. Fantini and Robert L. Sinclair, Eighty-fourth Yearbook of the National Society for the Study of Education (Chicago: University of Chicago Press, 1985), pp. 230–244.

42. Refer to chapter 3 for a description of "retreating" as a stage of seriousness in marginal behavior.

7

The School, the Principal, and the Marginal Student

The major responsibility of a public school is to help all young people learn. This concern for the development of all individuals is central to the effectiveness of our educational system and consistent with the expressed value that each student in a democratic society has an equal opportunity for a quality education. Yet a close look at reality in too many schools shows that students are sorted, and some are encouraged to excel while others become alienated and fall farther behind.[1] These young people who disconnect where others thrive become marginal students who are progressively relegated to the fringes of the school environment where there are fewer opportunities to achieve at high levels. It is not surprising that one perennial challenge facing elementary and secondary schools is the reform of environments for learning so that more students will benefit to a greater extent from public education. The educational leadership of the principal within the single school is crucial to meeting this challenge.

The effective school in a democracy is a self-renewing school—one that continually monitors its own progress, identifying and solving problems that interfere with the learning of students. Such schools are permeated by a "can-do" attitude based on confidence that the school community can steadily improve by reexamining its assumptions and modifying its practices. Concern for learners who are not successfully taking advantage of the school environment to learn is at the heart of a self-renewing school, for the desire to diagnose and the determination to solve student learning difficulties provide the impetus for ongoing improvement.

This chapter focuses on two critical aspects of the role of a principal in a self-renewing school. First, it is the role of the principal to articulate the public school mission of quality integrated education for all in terms of local conditions. Practically speaking, this involves encouraging teachers and school staff to believe in the capability of their learners and in their own ability to create vigorous ways for all students to learn. Schools that are consistently unsuccessful with their learners tend to be mired in a slough of restraining attitudes and counterproductive practices that defy efforts by students, parents, and educators to break the cycle of defeat and discouragement. Prior to problem solving in any school, but especially in schools that have a sizeable population of marginal students, it is the role of the principal to build a platform of shared concerns, positive attitudes, and common goals.

Second, the principal must lead educators and parents in accomplishing the school's mission with learners. The effective principal rallies teachers, parents, and interested members of the local community to identify specific problems their school is having in its attempt to educate all students. Discovering these problems for themselves builds common concern for improvement among members of this team. Also, the principal, in concert with the school-improvement team, develops and implements plans to reconstruct school environments so that increased learning will result for marginal students. As leader of this team, the principal facilitates constructive dialogue and inquiry with the total school staff about specific conditions in the school that might be hindering the learning of some students. Ralph Tyler reminds us that the principal's role is to help those who are closest to learners (teachers and parents) understand that improvement comes through solving problems that are special to their school. The inquiry into such problems and the attempts to solve them are powerful ways in which educational improvements do occur.[2]

In many cases, teams find that identification of problems and implementation of desired changes are dependent upon the extent to which educators redefine their thinking and roles with respect to marginal students. Specifically, the successful principal will lead teachers, both collectively and individually, to consider the need to personally redefine their ways of thinking about and interacting with marginal students.[3] The team will discover that marginal status is not justification for excluding the individual from activities that provide access to quality learning. However, it is also not enough simply to provide troubled learners with the same opportunities afforded the more successful students. Because of their deficit in achievement, the same treatment for marginal youth is not equal treatment. Rather, in order to counter the trend toward becoming marginal, it is necessary to create a personalized environment that may be more abundant so that it connects productively with the marginal learner.[4] The principal's leadership engages the teachers in inquiry about how changes in their responsibilities toward marginal students can be compelling dimensions of this reconstructed environment for learning.

As presented previously in chapter 4, there is substantial evidence that school conditions and teacher behavior can contribute to students' becoming marginal. Thus the role of the principal for initiating ongoing school improvement seems clear—to reduce marginality, the principal must lead the school community in examining and altering these critical aspects of the school environment. Yet school conditions and teacher behavior are rationalized and supported by traditions and beliefs that make them relatively insusceptible to influence. To penetrate the defenses surrounding many school practices that may be actually inducing or permitting marginal behavior, the principal and other school leaders must counter widely held views about assisting marginal learners that are restraining necessary school renewal.

It is the patterned ways that educators think about their responsibilities toward students that must be considered in order to realize lasting and meaningful improvements in curriculum and instruction. The ways educators think about their relations with marginal students affects how they behave toward these learners. Simply put, those views that contribute to constructive behavior

need to be maintained and those ways of thinking that contribute to
unconstructive behavior need to be adjusted so that principals and
teachers can be more effective in assisting all students to succeed.

RESTRAINING VIEWS TOWARD ASSISTING MARGINAL STUDENTS

Renewing public schools so that marginality can be reduced is
complex and demanding work because it involves leading people to
reconsider deeply held views and habits that are reinforced by
traditions of the school culture. At least five counterproductive
viewpoints that contribute to the reluctance or inability of schoolpeople to assist marginal learners are slowly being altered around
the country. To start and sustain a dialogue that challenges the
conventional wisdom educators have about marginal learners requires significant leadership within the school, leadership by the
principal.[5] The principal is not the only educator who provides
leadership; others may also lead because leadership is a function,
not a position.[6] Yet the principal is particularly crucial to a school
effort to alter thinking and initiate action so that those who are
closest to learners will actually reach more of them.[7] What are some
of the restraining views that may block efforts to assist marginal
students? We briefly describe here some of the most prevalent and
hindering viewpoints. These are advanced to provide a basis for
principals to recognize and challenge the conceptual constraints
that undermine constructive problem solving at the school level.

Marginal Behavior Is Ultimately the Student's Problem, Not the School's

Teachers' efforts to assist failing students are often conceived as
acts of compassion and concern for students' problems, or as
compensation for societal forces that place some youngsters at a
disadvantage. It is still a minority of teachers who hold to the view
that when a student fails, it is the school that has also somehow
failed because proper conditions for learning were not provided.
Most explanations for failure that begin "this child can't . . .,"
"this child won't . . .," "this child didn't . . .," direct the reason for

failure to the student without recognizing the shared responsibility of the teacher and the educational environment for both the problem of marginality and its solutions. Most school staffs are still in the paradoxical position of trying to fit their marginal individuals back into the ongoing environmental conditions that have partially caused the low performance in the first place. Students are blamed rather than organizations changed. Yet in some schools a sense of shared responsibility for marginal behavior is being shown by efforts to create physical, social, and intellectual conditions designed for all students to succeed, including those who are marginal.

Temporary Alienation Can Be a Necessary Stage in Learning

Another view that permeates the way too many educators think and is offered to rationalize the reluctance of principals and teachers to assist marginal learners is the assertion that coping individually with difficulties in school actually builds character and prepares one for future adversity. Confronting the limits of one's skills and knowledge at an early age is sometimes viewed as producing a deeper determination to overcome these limits. After all, the rugged individual will eventually learn that most institutions are unresponsive, so he or she must begin early to identify and use personal resources to prevail. This view might apply best to someone being trained to survive in the woods, but it is not appropriate for someone consistently lost in an institution that was purposefully established by society to foster meaningful learning for all individuals.

The forcing of inner-directed motivation through alienation may be effective with some mature learners who have previously experienced success, but its consequences may be disastrous for most students in difficulty who are searching for direction to get away from failure. For example, this way of thinking can be influencing the behavior of teachers who make up especially difficult tests to "show" students how high their standards are and to make them realize they will have to work harder and behave better to succeed in class. This is at best questionable behavior when it is known that only very few can rise to such a challenge. Although no student rises to low standards, the challenge should be rigorous enough to give students pleasure when they succeed and should be appropriately designed to build on the skills and strengths students possess.

Another example of the view that marginal status is the student's problem is reflected in school policies that force a student to remain in a class he or she has already failed rather than create an alternative and more appropriate environment for learning. Typically, when students remain in the environment where they failed, their behavior, motivation, and achievement do not improve, although cynicism may indeed increase.

This viewpoint is also expressed in the punitive element that creeps into teachers' demands for harsh punishment for some misbehaving students (usually those who are most deviant). Rejected in these terms, most students become more rather than less defiant—they become more established as marginal.

Finally, this way of thinking is responsible in part for systems of evaluation and grading that focus on criticism of students' mistakes rather than on encouragement and support for increasing their learning. The result of such negative approaches for those who are marginal is usually an increase in failure, not an increase in knowledge or confidence.

Temporary alienation can be a healthy stage in learning only if it stimulates outreach by educational environments. Students in difficulty need to be led back to firm foundations, and guided forward through experiences of success. Initially, this may imply reviewing previous skills or material and allocating more time for mastering new objectives presented in smaller increments. Students are sustained through temporary alienation by the support of their school, family, and communities, and by confidence based on experience that their skills can develop to face new challenges.

The Teacher's Primary Responsibility Is to Present and Cover Required Course Content: Learning Outcomes Are the Responsibility of the Student

From the time when the school curriculum was the primary means of providing information about the outside world to the student, teachers have viewed as their primary responsibility the coverage of course content. Indeed, curriculum improvement typically involves adopting a new textbook. This orientation to curriculum breeds a limited view of instruction that emphasizes the teacher's delivery of information to students.

In today's information-rich environments outside school settings, many educators are questioning the predominance of the traditional function of the curriculum and the continuation of teaching as simply delivering content to students. The view of students as receptacles to be filled leads to teachers who think that their job is done when the last of the required content has been presented. Teachers must search for ways to view the curriculum as a more flexible and responsive vehicle for encouraging each student to reach his or her academic potential.[8] Teachers who emphasize only the linear coverage of course content but do not promote a rich mixture of skills to process or internalize this content and the information presented in nonschool settings are likely to have in their classrooms more alienated learners. Such teaching implies a narrow band of preferred ways of learning that favor some individuals while they handicap others. Thus, the problem of marginal learners predictably increases whenever the curriculum swings to an overemphasis on covering content at the expense of teaching the thinking skills students need to learn content.[9]

Teachers Do Not Have the Time or the Responsibility to Correct Errors and Gaps in Student Learning That Have Resulted from Previous Years of Study

As students move from one teacher to another each hour, term, or year, the learning errors (and strengths) they have developed in one setting are compounded with the errors (and progress) they make in subsequent classrooms. Without clear-cut methods for identifying and monitoring gains and weaknesses in skills, without a systematic way of recording or communicating each teacher's perceptions of an individual's strengths and needs in learning, and without an adequate list of the prerequisite skills needed to begin a new subject, teachers find themselves in the perplexing situation of teaching blindly to groups of individuals who may diverge widely in their readiness for learning. Although a brief period of review is built into many courses, it is typically aimed at assisting students who have previously learned key skills.

Students who do not have the prerequisite skills necessary for success in a class are often forced to shift for themselves because the teacher thinks that attention given to these youngsters may detract from the learning of those students who are prepared or because the teacher simply does not have time to give marginal students the help they need. This either-or mentality comes in part from the fact that a teacher's contribution as a professional is often judged on how much the class learns in a set period of time. A teacher's view of the best investment of time can cause a marginal student to try to fill in the learning gaps while he or she simultaneously tries to keep up with the regular classwork—a situation in which the odds for success are slim. Simply put, a learner who lacks an appropriate preparation typically has great difficulty catching up. When teachers resist taking time from large-group instruction to reteach previous skills, students who want to overcome their handicaps must assertively seek out extra assistance at home, after school from their peers, or from independent study. Learners who are unable to find such assistance can become inexorably marginal in school.

A Marginal Student's Family Is Usually a Major Source of the Student's Problem

Unfortunately, parents of marginal learners are still generally considered a problem to the school. The view is that either they cannot be contacted when needed, they too are helpless before the student's troubles, or they are difficult because they have the nerve to challenge the school's labeling and treatment of the student. Usually parents are contacted by the school because their child is in trouble. Most of these communications between school and home still go formally through counselors or administrators. When the school deals with marginal learners, teachers and parents—the people closest to the learner—often maintain a great distance between each other, and when they do talk, little is said about the progress the student is making in his or her learning.

Although there is an urgent need to improve the learning of

marginal students, the family cannot be expected to bring about immediate changes in student performance. The persistent and complex problems of marginal students suggest that families should not be judged by their ability to create quick solutions. Professional educators need to expand their understanding of how families can educate. To this end, Hope Leichter suggests:

> . . . education in families cannot necessarily be improved by attempting to make it more like that in schools. Policies of increased homework, greater parental supervision, and encouragement of diligence, while they may be applicable to some families, are not based on an understanding of the complex dynamics of family life. They are narrowly directed toward enhancing those areas where education in families is similar to that in schools. This may well be appropriate in many instances, but it fails to take account of the rich and varied process by which education takes place within families.[10]

Deficits within their families may indeed contribute to students' weak academic performance. Yet the family can also be a powerful force for helping to correct the learning problems students experience.[11] This potential for promoting learning will not be tapped by investigating static variables such as the income or the education level of parents. Rather, consideration of the dynamic dimensions of the family setting will likely improve education within families and students' performance in schools. For example, schoolpeople and family members must work together to examine features of the home setting that are likely to contribute to learning, such as language interaction between children and adults, parents' aspirations for their children, organization of time and space, control over influences that might hinder learning, and links with other institutions or people who educate. These family variables are alterable; they can be purposefully created to help increase student learning.[12] Thus the school needs to support the idea that the family may be part of the long-term solution to a marginal student's problems.

One of the principal's critical responsibilities in preparing the school for improvement is to work with teachers so that these viewpoints about assisting learners who are disaffected can take on constructive dimensions. The viewpoints are vulnerable to analysis since they represent a contradiction between the responsibility of public schools to educate all students and the inability of some school staff to reach and teach a deserving population that has become marginal. When the viewpoints can be examined objectively, before the implied threat of implementing a specific program is at hand, most teachers will admit the contradiction and be more receptive to searching for new directions to solve school problems. The principal can introduce these directions both directly and indirectly: in rationales for disciplinary decisions; as background for explaining a curriculum revision; in conversations in the hall; in addresses to parents; in school publications, staff meetings, or in-service programs. The principal has a vast symbolic apparatus for conveying the school's mission. A critical leadership function is to interpret that mission in a way that challenges the cogency of viewpoints that hinder improvement.

Efforts to improve the complex links between the total school environment and learning also go beyond altering the views toward marginal students. Each school staff will have crucial problems that must be solved in its own setting in order to increase the performance of marginal students. Because student populations, teacher characteristics, and community demographics differ from school to school, the specific nature of the problems will also differ. This means that there is no single solution to the array of problems schools will identify. Rather, the differences across schools suggest that marginality as a national problem will be addressed by educators implementing solutions that emerge from an analysis of their own problems and a creative use of existing and additional resources.

Programs and agencies at federal, state, and district levels can prove helpful; but meaningful improvements for increasing student learning will be made by the individual school only.[13] The success of improvement programs initiated by agencies that are remote from the school is determined by the extent to which they link with what is being attempted in the local school. Significant and lasting improvements in the effectiveness of schools will not result from pressures of distant policies and lofty lists of priorities that do not connect to problems schools are encountering or assist with solutions staffs are implementing in their attempt to educate all students. The success of any serious effort to reconstruct the environment for learning depends upon the principal leading the teachers and interested community members in identifying and addressing significant problems that the individual school is having in increasing the learning of its students.

PROBLEM SOLVING IN THE SINGLE SCHOOL

The Coalition for School Improvement, consisting of diverse elementary and secondary schools in western Massachusetts, is one example of a program designed to support local educators in their efforts to identify and solve problems their schools are having in helping all students learn.[14] To launch school-improvement efforts, schools participating in the coalition are using the constructive side of the viewpoints we have discussed. Teachers and principals are examining their thinking toward marginal students, and local school teams are identifying problems and implementing possible solutions to increase student learning. The ongoing work of the demographically varied coalition schools illustrates the interrelated parts of a problem-solving process that is proving to be practical and sound. We do not mean this process to be prescriptive or definitive. Rather, knowledge of this process in actual use may stimulate other school staffs to engage in compelling discussions about ways they can improve student learning in their schools.

Indeed, the problem-solving process that a school staff uses to bring about improvements can take many forms. Yet our work with the coalition schools suggests that three basic steps in problem solving seem useful: identifying crucial problems, developing the action plan, and assessing progress. The improvement teams work through these interrelated parts of the process as they create an environment in their particular school that is intended to promote learning for their students.

Identifying Crucial Problems

The principal should guide the team to focus on a manageable number of significant problems that interfere with the learning of a considerable number of students. It is better to have a clear sense of one or two key problems rather than to take on an agenda that spreads the effort too thin and saps energy and resources dry so that little improvement is accomplished. The significant problems are identified by the team's inquiring into the academic strengths and weaknesses of their students. Identifying the strengths can help the team understand what needs to be maintained as they attempt to correct weaknesses of individual students or certain groups of students. Also, such identified strengths provide a positive base that can be used to overcome students' deficiencies. Awareness of students' strengths in learning contributes to a balance so that staff do not become so discouraged by problems that they think there is no possibility of being more successful with marginal students.

The principal's role is to help the team understand that identification of a few key problems does not mean that all is wrong with the school. The problems identified by analyzing the weaknesses of students can be of various types. For example, one elementary school team in the coalition considered that teachers' low expectations for a group of students from economically poor homes were contributing to the lack of success these students were having in learning to read. Another elementary school team reported that students were not achieving in social studies because the curriculum lacked clear objectives and the reading materials needed to be made more current so that they would spark the imagination and interest of the students. A high school team considered the way students were sorted for instruction into three ability groups to be counterproductive because students in the low groups were showing evidence of reduced motivation for learning. For these students, who were thought to be low achievers, there was an increase in absenteeism, an increase in discipline problems, and an increase in the dropout rate. Finally, a middle school team discovered through classroom observations that students did not express their ideas orally in an effective manner. The data collected in observations of English and history classes showed that students did not sequence their thoughts and did not use facts to support an argument. These are examples of problems that can be identified and solved so that learning can be increased.

Developing the Action Plan

The principal can lead the team in a detailed analysis of the problem in order to gather evidence of specific deficiencies in student achievement, consider reasons for these deficiencies, and explore possible changes in the school environment that are likely to reverse low achievement. For some problems it might be productive to consider changes that can be made in nonschool settings (particularly the home) in order to increase learning.

After a comprehensive analysis of the problem is completed and the resulting data are reviewed, the team may generate possible solutions to the problem. It is reasonable to anticipate that the analysis will reveal aspects of the problem that teachers, parents, and the principal can solve by altering their behavior or by changing conditions in the school or home. The data might also suggest that students need to improve the quality of their efforts to learn. Because of the various ways the problem can be attacked, it is not likely that only one solution will be advanced by the team. In order to select the solution that shows the most promise for succeeding, a pool of possible solutions can be generated and each one examined. Often the solution that has a substantial impact on solving the problem is one that includes all members of the team in its implementation.

For example, one team identified the poor writing skills of upper-grade students in an urban elementary school as a problem that needed attention. A comprehensive analysis of the problem revealed that teachers only occasionally gave assignments that required writing and students were seldom expected to turn in their written work. Hence, students were not practicing writing skills, and when they did write, their performance was not being evaluated. The team also discovered through interviews with students that the students did not understand why they needed to learn to write, and only a few students were motivated to improve their writing. The team discussed these aspects of the problem and proposed various solutions. After exploring advantages and disadvantages of each option, the team decided to redesign the curriculum to include visits to businesses and government agencies in the community so that students could see the practical uses of writing and to have students begin developing writing skills by writing and sending letters to friends, relatives, and famous people. Also, it was decided that teachers would participate in a staff-development program to improve their competencies in the teaching of the writing process.

After selecting a viable solution, the team develops a specific plan for implementation. This involves determining the changes to be made in the school environment and altering ways teachers relate to marginal students or other students. The sequence of actions likely to result in desired changes is detailed, and the schedule for implementation is determined. The team will estimate the time it will take to implement each part of the plan. It is crucial for the principal to help members of the team understand that changing the attitudes, skills, and behaviors of teachers and students will take longer than they might anticipate. Although some progress can be made in the initial years, successful implementation of the plan, meaningful modifications in how teachers relate to marginal students, and increased student learning may require five or more years.

After the schedule for the long-range plan is developed, the goals for the first year are set. The goals will state what improvements in student learning could be accomplished by the end of the first year and what parts of the plan could be implemented during this initial phase of improvement. These goals will tell the school staff where to direct their energy for improvement and provide the team with specific criteria for assessing progress.

Assessing Progress

Assessing the progress of the plan helps the team to determine whether or not the first-year goals for increased student learning are being accomplished. Also, the plan should be assessed periodically in order to make necessary changes in the plan's implementation or to adjust the plan's goals. If assessments of the attempts to improve student learning and to change school conditions show progress, the team can build on their strengths to implement the remaining parts of the plan.

It is important for the assessment to consider whether changes included in the plan, such as changes in the school's grouping practices, changes in teachers' relationships with marginal students, revisions in curriculum, and so on, are actually being implemented. If this information is not provided, it is difficult to determine the true impact of the plan on assisting students to learn. Also, the assessment needs to include data about student learning that go beyond the typical information collected in standardized tests. This means that samples of student work, teachers' reports of changes in learning, observations of student behavior, self-evaluations by students, and interviews with parents about changes in their children are useful sources of data for determining progress toward goals. When standardized tests are used to collect data for the assessment, care should be taken to assure that what is being tested relates to the goals for learning and to what the plan is attempting to accomplish. A mismatch between what is tested and what is being attempted to improve student learning can give the team inappropriate information about student progress or lead to changes in the plan that may misdirect the possible success of their long-term agenda. The principal's role in assessing progress is the same as in providing leadership for identifying school problems and developing the action plan; that is, the principal, as a participating member of the team, guides discussions and encourages teachers and others to make decisions and take constructive action.

One way, then, to determine the quality of a school is to look for how it treats students who are struggling in their learning. This emphasis on reaching marginal students taps the school's commitment to each individual's right to an equal opportunity for a quality education. Although all students may have a tendency to be marginal at some time, it is mostly the poor and ethnic and racial minorities who are at risk of failing in school. There is a high incidence of underachievement among these students who need an educational environment that helps correct their academic difficulties. Unfortunately, too many educators perceive that marginal students are low-ability students who do not have the motivation or capacity to succeed at school. Yet being marginal is not synonymous with low ability and permanent low achievement, or with any racial or economic group.

The principal and teachers working in concert in their single school to develop constructive ways of thinking about marginal students and to change practices that hinder student learning is indicative of a quality school. The varied approaches used to reach marginal students can be placed on a continuum of interactions between students and educators, with one end adjusting the educational environment to promote increased learning and the other insisting that performance in school can be improved by forcing students to conform to existing conditions. We suggest that the school staff that renews the educational environment to promote increased learning is more effective than the one that constantly seeks to prove that the problem of low achievement or marginality is the result of a deficiency or a weakness of the individual student. The quality school, then, strives to redesign the environment for learning instead of intensifying what exists and insisting that the marginal student adapt.

NOTES

1. Jeannie Oakes, *Keeping Track: How Schools Structure Inequality* (New Haven: Yale University Press, 1985).

2. Ralph W. Tyler, "The Role of the Principal in Promoting Student Learning" (Paper presented at the Massachusetts School Administrators Conference, Sturbridge, Mass., 1986), pp. 7–8.

3. For an analysis of how changing ways of thinking and how redefining roles serve as powerful interventions for increasing student learning, see Jim Cummins, "Empowering Minority Students: A Framework for Intervention," *Harvard Educational Review* 56 (February 1986): 18–36.

4. For an analysis of factors affecting an individual's success or failure in school learning, see John B. Carroll, "A Model of School Learning," *Teachers College Record* 64 (May 1963): 723–733.

5. For a process that uses student perceptions of curriculum conditions to stimulate this dialogue, see Ward J. Ghory and Robert L. Sinclair, "Thinking about Our School: The Environmental Perceptions Approach to Curriculum Inquiry and Improvement" (Paper presented at the Annual Meeting of the American Educational Research Association, San Francisco, 1979). ED 170–222.

6. It is possible to overstate the leadership function of the principal to make it appear that the principal is acting alone in school renewal. Frequently, a second change facilitator (an assistant principal; special teacher, or district supervisor) is nearly as active, and in some cases more active, than the principal. See Shirley Hord, Suzanne Stiegelbauer, and Gene Hall, "How Principals Work with Other Change Facilitators," *Education and Urban Society* 17 (November 1984): 89–109.

7. The crucial role of the principal in the local school is carefully and creatively discussed in John I. Goodlad, *A Place Called School: Prospects for the Future* (New York: McGraw-Hill, 1984), chap. 9, and in Ernest L. Boyer, *High School: A Report on Secondary Education in America* (New York: Harper and Row, 1983).

8. Neil Postman, *Teaching as a Conserving Activity* (New York: Delacorte Publishing Co., 1980).

9. Edward C. McDill, Gary Natriello, and Aaron M. Pallas, "Raising

Standards and Retaining Students: The Impact of the Reform Recommendations on Potential Dropouts," Reprint No. 358 (Baltimore: Center for Social Organization of Schools, Johns Hopkins University, 1985).

10. Hope Jensen Leichter, "Families as Educators," in *Education in School and Nonschool Settings*, ed. Mario D. Fantini and Robert L. Sinclair, Eighty-fourth Yearbook of the National Society for the Study of Education (Chicago: The University of Chicago Press, 1985), p. 99.

11. Barbara K. Iverson and Herbert J. Walberg, "Home Environment and Learning: A Quantitative Synthesis" (Paper presented at the Annual Meeting of the American Educational Research Association, San Francisco, 1979). In general, the home environmental process variables, when combined, correlated +0.70 to +0.80 with measures of school achievement involving reading, vocabulary, and problem solving.

12. Robert Sinclair and Ward J. Ghory, "Parents and Teachers Together: Directions for Developing Equality in Learning through Environments in Families and Schools," in *A Two-Way Street: Home-School Cooperation in Educational Decision Making*, ed. Robert L. Sinclair (Boston: Institute for Responsive Education, 1980), pp. 29–51.

13. Theodore R. Sizer, *Horace's Compromise* (Boston: Houghton Mifflin, 1984), pp. 214–215.

14. For a description of the purposes and organization of the Coalition for School Improvement, see "The Coalition for School Improvement: Working Together to Increase Learning," *Connecting* (Newsletter of the Center for Curriculum Studies, School of Education, University of Massachusetts, Amherst) 1 (Winter 1986): 1–2.

8

Families and Schools Together: Teaming to Support Marginal Learners

If we could look at family and school surroundings through the eyes of marginal students, we might see more clearly how to promote responsive educational environments and achieve greater equality in student learning. Children and youth have opportunities to observe varied conditions in each setting and to realize the impact of both spheres of influence. Parents can have access to views of the schooling landscape, and teachers can have access to views of the home environment; thus the groups can learn from each other. However, too often strained communication, conflicting roles, and other persistent barriers separate the adults from each other's domains. Although parents and teachers have collective responsibility for the education of young people, seldom do they share a mutual grip on family and school environments that can tap the potential all students have for learning, particularly those who are marginal.

Educators who are working to align home and school environments must realize that there are counterproductive aspects of the present relationship between families and schools. For example, conditions in both settings often work at cross purposes so that what students accomplish in one place is stifled or unlearned in the other. It is important for parents and teachers to join together to eliminate dysfunctional aspects of learning environments, to

141

reinforce conditions that have a positive impact, to maintain contrasts that contribute to academic competence, and to create new blends that encourage learning.

There is mounting evidence that the family is vital to and intimately linked with learning in school.[1] Yet family environment is seldom reflected in curriculum development. To ignore this homeground is to overlook variables that can be altered to increase marginal students' ability to learn.[2]

Typically, the solution to inadequate academic stimulation in the family has been to bring the child into school at an earlier age in order to compensate for the lack of education provided by parents. This approach suggests that parents and the conditions in families are the problem rather than part of the solution for educating children. Creating a separate preschool curriculum without improving or altering variables in the family environment can generate academic and cultural contradictions that hinder learning.

Many preschool educators are aware of this potential problem. To enable all students to learn at high standards, educators might revitalize rather than replace the contributions of the family. We are not suggesting that the family should remake itself in the image of the school, or vice versa. Instead, we are arguing that both places can become more effective in educating youth. Parents and teachers can work together to make each environment better and, in the process, build the conditions that increase learning as the student experiences both spheres of influence. To that end, we suggest two major directions for improving the family-school relationship and thus developing productive environments for increasing the learning of marginal students. First, we examine some existing viewpoints about education that separate families from schools. Second, we propose an approach for teaming parents and teachers, one that would encourage both groups to collaborate in building complementary learning environments for countering the learning difficulties of marginal students.

VIEWPOINTS SEPARATING PARENTS AND EDUCATORS

As professional educators assume increasing responsibility for children's learning outside the family, a way of thinking can develop that stresses separation between family and school. In schools, as in hospitals, a prevalent expectation holds that education, like health, is a service provided by professionals when the client visits an institutional setting. In both instances, parents often depend upon the professionals and their delivery of services, rather than provide a preventive, corrective, or supportive environment in the home. Clearly, this way of thinking must be reexamined when certain client groups or individuals fail to thrive under the institution's care. To this end, we review some common and possibly disabling viewpoints often held by parents and teachers about their roles in the educational process and suggest more-constructive alternative views. The purpose here is to build a foundation for an expanded way of thinking about the contributions of families and schools to the education of children and youth who are not realizing academic success.

Academic Competence Results from Successful Completion of Tasks Under the Direction of a Schoolteacher

This viewpoint suggests that the response to students who consistently are not learning would be to provide more classroom instruction, either at an earlier age or for extended periods of time. These can be considered compensatory strategies, which have been tried with some success in recent years.

However, the impact of early intervention programs can be boosted by emphasizing outreach to the family.[3] Evaluations of early-intervention programs that are family-centered suggest that the parents' provision of educational experiences has a long-term effect upon academic achievement.[4] Indeed, evidence shows that language development is an important basis for academic competence, that it begins during infancy, and that it can be influenced in a major way during the preschool and early school years. The data also show that experiences in the family are important factors in language development. Family education of young children is thus a major contributor to the development of academic competence.[5]

If development of academic concepts and skills is viewed as being promoted by the family as well as by the school, then attention is given to collaboration between the settings. The frame of reference used in developing programs to increase academic competence changes from an emphasis only on classroom intervention to one of cooperation between the family and school. Classroom teachers may coordinate their curriculum with parents or guardians who are working to educate their own children. The constructive view would be that academic competence results from successful completion of a broad range of activities both in families and in schools, particularly as these activities are reinforced through the interactions of the student with both parents and teachers.

Teachers Are Primarily Responsible for Decisions About the Academic (Mainly Cognitive) Growth of Children in School, While Parents Are Expected to Make Major Decisions About the Physical, Social, and Emotional Development of Their Children

One reason for the general failure of parents and teachers to work jointly on improving conditions for learning in families and schools is the assumption that they have basically different responsibilities. In effect, teachers and parents think that there are few decisions they can or should make together. This view leads each group to retreat to and defend separate spheres of territory and control.[6] When teachers assume sole responsibility for academic growth, they turn the classroom into a setting where they can make and implement decisions without fear of parental interference. If teachers welcome parents into their classrooms, they usually ask them to observe or to perform mundane chores. Their presence is considered temporary and peripheral to the classroom experiences of students. In the same way, parents create an inviolate space within their families, with customs and traditions teachers are generally not permitted to view or to participate in, much less question. As a result, parents often refrain from visiting the school, because it is hard to accept being excluded from a part of their youngster's world. So, too, teachers rarely visit families, where they presumably have no appropriate role.

However, when teachers acknowledge that parents have important information about students and can make lasting contributions to the development of academic competence, a basis for working together can be created. A recent review of twenty-four pilot and experimental programs makes it clear that family-based reinforcement of students' behavior in school is proving to be an efficient and effective method for motivating students to overcome some of their most persistent learning difficulties.[7] When parents' and families' possible contributions to increased academic competence are recognized, a more dependable position can be developed about the sharing of decision-making responsibilities. As the persons who are closest to the learner, parents and teachers together should design and implement educational environments to assist students in their cognitive, affective, and physical development in the family and the school.

The Important Variables in the Family That Affect Academic Competence Are Essentially Unalterable

This way of thinking grants the importance of the family environment, but denies that variables in the family can be changed. For years, study after study of the sources of academic achievement attempted to correlate academic success or failure with relatively unalterable variables like cultural background, socio-economic status (as measured by parental education, income, or occupation), family size, sibling order, and so on.[8] Attempts were also made to relate intelligence measures to the same variables, which suggests that conditions that influence the learner in the family are givens with which educators must cope.

However, in the last twenty years research approaches that emphasize alterable variables thought conducive to learning suggest that specific activities parents do with their children can have a direct influence on academic competence. Some of the variables that have been examined include encouragement of children to learn well, parental aspirations, provision of help for learning, and organization of time and space for study. Recently, Barbara Iverson and Herbert Walberg conducted a quantitative synthesis of eighteen studies of the family environments of 5,831 youth in eight countries. They found that parent stimulation of the child in the family showed a consistently stronger relationship with intelligence, motivation, and achievement than did the measures of socioeconomic status.[9] The family variables measured by these studies are changeable; they have been identified as aspects of the environment that can be readily influenced by programs to support parents' efforts to improve family settings.[10] The evolving view now is that the important variables in the family environment that affect academic competence can be altered to increase students' learning.

The Organizational Conditions That Hinder Teachers from Including Home Environment as Part of the Curriculum Are Practically Impossible to Influence from Inside the School

In their hierarchical organizations, educators typically see change coming from outside their own realm of control. For example, teachers look to the principals or to the department heads for the schedule; principals turn to the central office for curriculum; and central-office administrators approach the school board for new policy guidelines. Given this practice of looking elsewhere, educators' ability to assume responsibility for improvement, as well as their feelings of competence and security, is undermined at each level. When this happens, educators tend to use the organizational variables they do control as protection against outside suggestions or assistance for improvement. Paradoxically, an educator may feel a certain comfort when others are responsible for change, even when he or she is dissatisfied with current conditions. The comfort seems to come from knowing that an outsider is accountable for school improvement and, at the same time, is not as knowledgeable as an insider about the conditions that need to be altered in order to increase student learning.

Despite their initial protests to the contrary, teachers and school administrators will acknowledge that what happens in the classroom or school depends primarily upon them. While change in organizational conditions may be limited or directed by decision makers outside the school, the persons who bear responsibility for and actually implement improvements are those who are inside. Improvements in curriculum and instruction depend upon local expertise and the ability of teachers and principals to respond to particular conditions in their own schools.

It is unlikely, however, that genuine efforts to include parents in curriculum development will be effective unless a shift occurs concerning the responsibility for change borne by the people closest to the teaching and learning process. There are schools that effectively combine family and school environments in curriculum planning. Further, there are organizational means to permit parents and teachers to communicate about ways to help students learn.[11] But unless educators support and encourage the individuals who want to take responsibility for altering the organizational conditions that hinder collaboration, the school will continue to breed system loyalists who use the institution as a protection against improvement by shifting the responsibility for change to outsiders who cannot implement improvements without them. The assumption that schools cannot be improved from within to permit parents and teachers to collaborate must be revised as part of an expanded way of thinking about the potential partnership of the family and school. Effectiveness with marginal learners requires that teachers and administrators provide leadership from inside the school to develop curriculum that appropriately combines family and school environments.

Correcting these viewpoints that can separate families and schools opens the way to considering appropriate teaming of parents and teachers. Both groups must reconsider and revise some persistent assumptions and realize that academic competence is fostered both in families and in schools, that parents and teachers both have an appropriate role in making decisions about the child's development, that variables in the family environment related to improving learning can be altered, and that the school can be reorganized from within to promote cooperation with the family. Most likely, agreement on revised views will be reached gradually, as the result of shared practical experiences in mutual projects designed to increase student learning. Such teaming will occur informally and sporadically at first as means for cooperation and communication develop. We propose in the next section of this chapter a design that we think may help translate these expanded ways of thinking into constructive decisions about creating family and school environments for learning.

DESIGN FOR TEACHER-PARENT TEAMING

Organized efforts by schools to involve parents can be categorized according to the roles schools expect parents to play.[12] The parents' most common role is as an *audience*. They hear about the school through newsletters, at PTA meetings, or during visits to the school. Second, parents work in schools as *volunteers*, who assist as teacher aides or student chaperones. Third, parents are involved in schools as paid paraprofessional *employees*, often with a responsibility for organizing parent or community involvement programs. Fourth, parents have often participated as *policymakers*, frequently in an advisory capacity at the local school or in a legislative capacity as members of school boards. Fifth, parents are involved as direct and active *teachers* of their children in the family. Typically, parent education programs focus on helping parents learn more-effective ways of working with their children.

These roles for parent involvement frequently create a certain distance between parents and teachers. Often, an implied superior-inferior relationship surfaces, sometimes with parents in control as policymakers, sometimes with educators dictating to parental audiences about how to instruct in the home. Rarely do parents and teachers collaborate with similar status and responsibilities. The missing role of parent-teacher teams for increasing students' learning in families and schools may explain why so few parents maintain their involvement with schools. Parents who do attend scheduled parent-teacher conferences usually have children who are successful in school.[13] Further, volunteer programs have been found to attract parents who have positive attitudes and sophisticated child management skills to begin with.[14] These findings suggest that until parents and teachers can find ways to collaborate more as equals and bring different strengths and data to the shared task of helping students learn, parent programs organized through the school will reach only a narrow audience.

Teaming, then, is one possible direction for promoting more-productive mergers between parents and teachers. We suggest an approach for teaming that includes four key educational functions as one way to center parent-teacher collaboration on the increased learning of students. In brief, the functions are: building a shared platform of educational values and expectations that establishes reasons for learning and guides the teaching process; diagnosing a student's learning needs and characteristics to determine favorable curriculum conditions; planning and implementing environments that will make desired learning possible; and evaluating the effectiveness of the learning environments that are created in families and schools. We will explain each function, but we give more in-depth consideration to the third function (planning and implementing environments) because of its practical implications for revitalizing the home learning environment and improving the school curriculum.

Building a Platform

First, and most fundamentally, parents and teachers can team to build a shared platform of educational values and expectations that will shape the conditions they create for learning. Teachers need to understand the power and importance of the informal educational processes used in the families and communities of their marginal students. For example, parents can help teachers to appreciate unfamiliar cultural views and values. In the process, the teachers may become more responsive to the adaptations that youth from any highly personalized culture must make to cope with the more regulated forms and standardized procedures of school bureaucracies. If teachers can learn from parents about their students' cultures, then they can adjust the school environment to take advantage of the informal variables that are a critical part of the way the student perceives and learns. As Basil Bernstein puts it, if the culture of the teacher is to become part of the consciousness of the child, then the culture of the child must first be in the consciousness of the teacher.[15]

When parents send their children to a school that does not mirror the values and traditions of the child's family and community life, they apprehensively make an implicit deal with the teacher. In this arrangement the teacher is to provide students with opportunities to learn skills and attitudes necessary for success in the mainstream culture. However, these opportunities can come at a dear price for many parents and children. To master and internalize necessary academic and social skills, many youngsters must "make themselves over" to a degree, by altering their speech patterns, by reconsidering certain values, or by relaxing some previous connections to family and peers. Unless parents and teachers can reach some agreements on the importance of school

learnings and the style in which they are presented, the arrangement can become a painful ordeal for the student. It can lead to a
sense of not belonging in school or in the family.

The purpose for communication between parent and teacher
about an educational platform is to allow both to enter the partnership with greater confidence. With mutual support, the students
involved can meaningfully expand their skills and aspirations,
authentically blending the cultural gifts and environmental
strengths represented by the family and school into a personally
satisfying set of competencies and values. The greater the difference
between family culture and school norms, the greater the need for
parents and teachers to work at establishing a common platform of
shared educational values and expectations. From such under-
standings between parents and teachers, the student can make
some sense out of conflicting worlds at home and school; without
this understanding students might be forced into an either-or
choice between the two settings. But the building of a common
platform has often been neglected, and in most cases parents and
teachers must start at the very beginning. As Sara Lawrence Lightfoot puts it,

> Because they come together as strangers who share in the common task
> of education and socialization [teachers and parents] must engage in a
> relatively self-conscious and painstaking task of discovering each other.
> The process of learning about each other's values, styles and modes of
> communication may take relatively obscure and trivial forms at first, as
> parents, teachers and children begin to feel each other out. But the real
> message is not trivial; it is the initial phase of learning to act and interact
> in an authentic and meaningful way.[16]

In short, the first and most fundamental educational function
that can be accomplished through parent-teacher teaming is the
establishment of informal and formal agreements about appropriate learning for children and youth. Another way to put this is that
parents and teachers will come to share a common view of their
educational mission. Instead of plugging parents into prescribed
roles in already developed school programs, the school needs first
to involve parents in determining the reasons for education. We
believe a foundation for learning that both family and school

support can develop if parents and teachers take the necessary time and personal initiative to work as a team.

Diagnosing Students' Needs

Parents and teachers can also team to diagnose a student's specific learning needs and characteristics. The purpose of this part of the approach for teaming is to determine the skills and content to be learned and to identify how the student learns best. Parents who are knowledgeable of the student's behavior in a context outside school can provide a corrective check and balance to a school-based diagnosis. It is important to blend results from paper-and-pencil instruments or classroom observations by teachers with insights of parents who sample, through ongoing observations and informal talks, a wider range of behavior in the family setting. Through discussions parents can learn more about developmental stages and the structure of subject matter, and they can provide teachers with clues that might hold the key to unlocking the student's motivation to learn. If academic competence is a mixture of mastery of prerequisite skills with a desire to learn well, the different viewpoints and data that parents and teachers can share may enrich their mutual understanding of the student and improve the effectiveness of their efforts to increase learning.

Planning and Implementing Environments for Learning

With academic strengths and weaknesses and personal characteristics of students identified, the resulting data are used to plan a curriculum. This expressed curriculum consists of conditions or variables that are implemented in family and school environments through the efforts of parents and teachers. Of course, specific environmental variables and their varied degrees of intensity are arranged in either setting according to the individual learners. It is possible, however, to identify some positive conditions of families that are alterable and thus can be developed as part of the curriculum. These general conditions might also be considered appropriate for encouraging learning in school environments.

Bloom points out that in recent years more attention has been given to studies on improving environmental conditions in families.

These studies have looked into use of home visitors, special courses for parents, parent involvement in the school for brief periods of time, and the provision of audio-visual and written materials and instructional games to be used at various points in the student's development. This research shows that what parents do with children can be influenced and that the effects of such changes on school learning are meaningful.[17] The alterations parents make in their behavior toward their children can be considered to be curricula designed purposefully to promote academic competence. Bloom identifies the following as some of the environmental variables that can be mutually planned by parents and teachers and implemented in families: contribution of parents to language development, encouragement of children to learn well, aspirations of parents for their children, provision of help in learning when the child most needs it, and ways in which time and space are organized.[18] Bloom goes on to state,

> Such variables, when combined, correlate +0.70 to +0.80 with measures of school achievement. In general, the correlations are highest with school achievement involving reading, vocabulary, and problem solving and lowest with spelling and arithmetic computation. These results suggest that the home has greatest influence on the language development of the child, his general ability to learn, and his motivation to learn well in school. The home has least influence on specific skills primarily taught in the school.[19]

It is clear, then, that curriculum in the family can be altered, can contribute to learning, and needs to be complemented by curriculum in the school. That is, the school can support the family learning emphases and, at the same time, add conditions that assist students to master particular academic skills. One knotty problem schools confront when they develop a complementary environment is that while parents usually concentrate on individuals, teachers primarily interact with groups. The situation of individuals within groups requires that teachers try not to interact with students in ways that benefit some students but not others. Although it is possible to organize schools so that a single teacher engages with an individual student, the persistent reality is that a teacher faces a group. Solid attempts to meet individual differences in this sensitive setting can be supported by the larger school environment.

Experience suggests to us that there are variables of teacher-student interaction in schools that might make a difference in academic success for all learners, and particularly for marginal learners. It is likely that these variables, similar to those in the family, can be developed. The context for teaching and learning would be characterized by setting a clear expectation of excellence for all students, providing help in learning when students need it most, placing an emphasis on caring about the personal welfare of students, providing positive reinforcement and encouragement for learning, and collaborating with parents for learning in the family. A teacher would engage with a student within an environment that is intended to provide equal access to learning for all. A teacher would strive to ensure that students have both equality of educational opportunity and quality outcomes.

This third function has special importance because it also includes some practical ways in which parents and teachers can work together to implement environments that include the family and school. Consider, for example, implementation of some structured opportunities for learning and specific practices for reinforcement of desired behavior.

Structured opportunities allowing students to interact with a wide variety of people and sources of stimulation can contribute to meaningful language development.[20] For example, measures of academic competence in language are likely to increase when teachers and parents provide supplemental books, take the student to the library or bookmobile, work with plants or gardens, cook together, discuss friends and experiences, or share organized activities like story telling or recreation.[21] Another example of a practical family-school effort is the provision of "home learning recipes" developed by teachers to be implemented by parents. These are specific, no-cost, written activities designed to reinforce and supplement instruction in school. When used by families regularly, these basic skills activities have contributed to improved scores in reading and mathematics.[22]

Parents and teachers can also team to improve the organization of time and space to study. If a student is provided with time and space to study and with work that he or she can complete, an increase in the amount of time spent on learning tasks is likely to pay dividends in improved learning. A further example of a structured opportunity to encourage learning is the development of an early warning system in which parents and teachers inform each other when they see signs that the student needs extra help. As Bloom notes, the provision of help when the student most needs it is an obvious way to avoid the development of learning errors.[23]

In addition to structuring specific learning opportunities, parents and teachers can team to implement reinforcement practices that motivate students to learn and behave well. Adults should agree to some extent about how they will reward students for effective learning; that is, they should decide on the variety, frequency, and amount of reinforcement they plan to provide. One direct way to provide reinforcement is for parents and teachers to target specific academic skills that need improvement and then to schedule practices in the home and the school that will foster the desired behaviors. In his review of twenty-four studies and projects using this approach, Richard Barth reports consistent improvement on even the most persistent learning problems.[24]

In another series of studies of the learning environments of families that encourage high achievement, Bernard Rosen suggests that two kinds of family socialization practices—"achievement training" and "independence training"—generate motivation for achievement.[25] Rosen's major conclusion is that the psychological impetus to excel in situations involving standards of excellence comes from practice and support in similar situations. Parents and teachers, then, can promote high achievement by setting standards of excellence and by rewarding the student's persistence, concentration, and industriousness in reaching these levels. While achievement training aims to get children and youth to do things well, independence training attempts to teach them to do things on their own. In this latter training, parents and teachers can reach an agreement on how much the environment should stress individual or collective behavior and how much a future or a present orientation will be promoted. These decisions may be complex and difficult, but they are likely to be necessary to prevent family and school environments from working at cross-purposes.

The third function of parent-teacher teaming is perhaps the broadest and most open-ended. The identification and implementation of desired family and school variables moves the idea of curriculum as environments for learning into practical operation.

Evaluating Environments

The fourth suggested function of the approach for teaming is the evaluation of the learning environments created in families and schools. The function encourages parents and teachers to confirm the values of their efforts or to question and revise their initial ideas developed as a platform. Further, evaluating the environmental conditions they have decided upon and implemented together also provides teachers and parents with a responsibility for visiting each other's setting. Observing an aspect of the environment such as a quiet study area in home or classroom that has been designed for a specific purpose provides an opportunity to demonstrate what has been accomplished and to be receptive to praise and to additional ideas. Hence, it becomes possible to build on the positive. Like any learners, parents and teachers need opportunities to visualize and confirm their progress. This part of the design for teaming provides information about the effectiveness of the family and the school environments for promoting learning, and thus furnishes data that parents and teachers can use while working together to improve conditions in either setting. The evaluation function assists adults to determine, through direct observation and informal discussion, if what was planned for altering family and school settings was actually implemented. The joint evaluation would also include testing and observation of students to indicate academic gains that were accomplished during an established time period. Hence, parents and teachers would keep informed about what was learned well and what still needs to be learned. If approached as a means for improvement, evaluation can be an occasion for generating a renewed effort to accomplish a common purpose of developing environments to increase learning for all students.

This approach, then, includes four interrelated functions for helping children and youth learn. Through teaming, parents and teachers move from building a platform of values and expectations to determining learning needs, to planning and implementing environments, to evaluating the effectiveness of conditions in families and school. We are suggesting that teaming to carry out these functions is a missing element in parents' and teachers' current roles in educating students. It is anticipated that successful teaming will help narrow the separation between parents and teachers and thereby reduce the number of marginal students.

Despite increasing knowledge of the joint influence of families and schools on learning, educators are not yet fully exploring ways in which parents and teachers can support each other. As a result, school curriculum is often developed without considering family conditions. The school environment and the home environment are treated as separate entities. This is unfortunate because we think the coming together of families and schools is a powerful means for improving learning for marginal students who are not succeeding in the existing school curriculum. Bloom adds,

> It is clear that when the home and the school have congruent learning emphases, the child has little difficulty in his later school learning. But when the home and the school have divergent approaches to life and to learning, the child is likely to be penalized severely by the school—especially when school attendance is required for ten or more years.[26]

Students are often left alone to make sense out of the serious differences between the places where they are expected to live and to learn. The separation between families and schools can result in young people being torn between their loyalties to one place and the demands of another. However, they do not need to experience an unnecessary mismatch. Parents and teachers are starting to realize the success and benefits students receive when families and schools work together to promote academic achievement.

A common bond between parents and teachers seldom develops naturally or spontaneously. Hence, one priority in the years ahead will be leadership that can bring these adults together as a constructive force for helping all students learn, particularly those who are marginal. Parents' and teachers' concern for young people is a shared commitment that can bring them together. By working as a team, the family and the school may ensure that marginal students will receive opportunities for equality in learning.

NOTES

1. Three recent comprehensive reviews of literature on the impact of home environment on school performance support this contention with primarily correlational evidence from eight countries and approximately sixty studies. Each review calls for experimental investigation of specific models of parent and teacher cooperation as a way to extend the correlational implications of current work. See James Filipcazk, Ann Lordeman, and Robert M. Friedman, *Parental Involvement in the Schools: Towards What End?* (Silver Spring, Md.: Institute for Behavioral Research, 1977); Barbara Goodson and Robert Hess, *Parents as Teachers of Young Children: An Evaluative Review of Some Contemporary Concepts and Programs* (Palo Alto: Stanford University, 1975); and Barbara K. Iverson and Herbert J. Walberg, "Home Environment and Learning: A Quantitative Synthesis" (Paper presented at the Annual Meeting of the American Educational Research Association, San Francisco, 1979).

2. For examples of variables in home and classroom environments that are likely to influence school achievement, see Benjamin S. Bloom, "The New Direction in Educational Research: Alterable Variables" (Paper adapted from Bloom's *All Our Children Learning: A Primer for Parents, Teachers, and Other Educators* [New York: McGraw-Hill, 1981] and presented at the Invitational Conference on Testing, Educational Testing Service, Princeton, N.J., 1979).

3. Earl S. Schaeffer, "Enhancing Competence in the Classroom: A Developmental Perspective" (Paper presented at the Conference on the Human Dimension of Education, Albuquerque, N.M., 1980), p. 5.

4. Urie Bronfenbrenner, *A Report on Longitudinal Evaluations of Preschool Programs*, vol. 2, *Is Early Intervention Effective?* (Washington, D.C.: Department of Health, Education, and Welfare, 1974).

5. Earl S. Schaeffer, "Parents as Educators: Evidence from Cross-Sectional, Longitudinal, and Intervention Research," *Young Children* 27 (April 1972): 227–239.

6. Sara Lawrence Lightfoot, *Worlds Apart: Relationships between Families and Schools* (New York: Basic Books, 1978), pp. 25–30.

7. Richard Barth, "Home-Based Reinforcement of School Behavior: A Review and Analysis," *Review of Educational Research* 49 (Summer 1979): 436–458.

8. Karl Raymond White, "The Relationship between Socioeconomic Status and Academic Achievement" (Doct. diss., University of Colorado, 1976). This dissertation reviews one hundred studies relating socioeconomic status (SES) and achievement. In general, correlations of +0.30 to +0.50 were found between SES and achievement. See also, Herbert J. Walberg and Kevin Marjoribanks, "Family

Environment and Cognitive Development: Twelve Analytic Models," *Review of Educational Research* 46 (Fall 1976): 527–551.

9. Iverson and Walberg, "Home Environment and Learning." In general, the home environmental process variables, when combined, correlated +0.70 to +0.80 with measures of school achievement involving reading, vocabulary, and problem solving.

10. Lawrence Dolan, "The Affective Consequences of Home Support, Instructional Quality, and Achievement," *Urban Education* 13, no. 3 (1978): 323–343.

11. Some popular organizational strategies for this purpose include hiring an additional staff person as a liaison between families and schools; organizing a school so that teams of teachers teach the same group of students and divide the responsibility to contact homes; and sending notes home on a regular basis to report progress on specific behaviors targeted by parents and teachers as priorities.

12. Ira J. Gordon, *Parent Involvement in Compensatory Education* (Urbana, Ill.: University of Illinois Press, 1970), p. 7.

13. Kenneth N. Anchor and Feliciz N. Anchor, "School Failure and Parental School Involvement in an Ethnically Mixed School: A Survey," *Journal of Community Psychology* 2, no. 3 (1974): 265–267.

14. Merle V. Karnes and R. Reid Zehrback, "Parental Attitudes and Education in the Culture of Poverty," *Journal of Research and Development in Education* 8, no. 2 (1975): 44–53.

15. Basil Bernstein, *Class, Codes, and Control*, vol. 1 (London: Routledge and Kegan Paul, 1971), p. 199.

16. Lightfoot, *Worlds Apart*, p. 189.

17. Bloom, "The New Direction in Educational Research," p. 14.

18. Ibid., p. 13.

19. Ibid.

20. Trevor Williams, "Abilities and Environments," in *Schooling and Achievement in American Society*, ed. William H. Sewell, Robert M. Hauser, and David L. Featherman (New York: Academic Press, 1976), pp. 66–67.

21. Earl S. Schaeffer and M. Edgerton, "Parent Interview and Sociodemographic Predictors of Adaptation and Achievement" (Paper presented at the American Psychological Association Annual Conference, New York, 1979).

22. Dorothy Rich, Beverly Mattox, and James Van Dien, "Building on Family Strengths: The 'Non-Deficit' Involvement Model for Teaming Home and School," *Educational Leadership* 36 (April 1979): 506–510.

23. Bloom, "The New Direction in Educational Research."

24. Barth, "Home-Based Reinforcement of School Behavior."

25. Bernard C. Rosen, "Race, Ethnicity, and the Achievement Syndrome," *American Sociological Review* 24 (February 1959): 47–60.

26. Bloom, "The New Direction in Educational Research," p. 13.

9

Toward School Renewal: Premises for Dialogue and Action

Attending to marginal students is at the crux of lasting school renewal. For more than incremental improvement to occur in schools, we must reach the students on the margins. Any other approach to improving schools may prove divisive, thereby increasing the gap between those who benefit and those who do not achieve to their potential. Valuable short-term gains in achievement or readiness for college may be accomplished by strategies demanding more from the few students sorted into the top track, but the long-term agenda is for American public schools to help more of their students succeed at high levels.

We think the problems of marginal students may be addressed best where they most often emerge—in local schools. The same pedagogic strategies and environmental adjustments needed to help teachers relate more effectively with marginal learners are also promising approaches for adaptive and productive instruction that will benefit all learners. In other words, the insights gained from helping learners in difficulty may provide constructive directions for encouraging other learners to increase their achievement. For this reason, looking to the margins is essential to school improvement. The teacher who is capable with marginal students has attitudes and skills that are likely to work well with all learners.

Moreover, the process of dialogue and problem solving that

159

school staffs undertake to unravel the knotty problems experienced by marginal students is needed to transform relatively static school environments into self-renewing settings. Instead of implementing a packaged instructional program developed externally to the school and rationalized by a new orthodoxy, school staffs need to set into motion an ongoing process of introspection, analysis, and improvement. In the crucible of a student crisis are endless possibilities for responses. By returning again and again to examine breakdowns and breakthroughs in the ways students relate to particular school and classroom environments, a school staff develops analytic skills and a technical repertoire for continuing improvement. The "shake and bake" mentality for quick, one-step problem solving is replaced by professional dialogue, planning, and action that strives for quality rather than for compromise and convenience.

As we see it, educators today are forced to consider the margins in order to develop an incisive perspective about the effectiveness of their institution in providing an equal and a quality education. Facing honestly the evidence of underachievement and squandered potential in schools prevents educators from becoming complacent about ongoing conditions in schools that may channel too many students into unproductive patterns of behavior. As a sensitizing force heightening critical awareness of hitherto neglected issues, the problems of marginal students should be at the center of attention of educators responsible for renewing public schools.

STARTING WITH THE LOCAL SCHOOL

The proliferation of education reports now coming from national studies and state commissions is generating what seems to be an unending list of recommendations for reform that schoolpeople are expected to implement. These "should do" lists for teachers, principals, superintendents, and interested members of the community are usually detailed in the last chapter of the report. The hundreds of recommendations to prepare American schools for the changes and challenges of contemporary times are well intended and usually carefully developed. Yet the unavoidable we-know-what-you-should-do tune that resonates from such a list is seldom appreciated by those who face the reality in schools and classrooms day after day. This externally developed agenda for improvement seems to be "legislated action" by a source remote from the actual problems of a particular elementary or secondary school. Hence, the recommendations are often perceived by school staffs to be out of joint with their own necessary agenda.

The lists of priorities directed to all schools appear to ignore the fact that schools are different from one another in significant ways. We think that in order for improvement efforts to be meaningful and lasting, the changes need to link with the specific problems a local school is experiencing in its attempts to increase student learning. The directions for improvement need to originate with educators inside the institution, not from a distant source that enjoys the luxury of not being accountable for its suggestions that someone else has to implement. This does not mean that those inside the schools have all the answers, or that those outside the schools do not contribute a great deal to the insiders' decision making. The point is that those professional educators who are closest to learners are the key leaders for school renewal.

The contradiction between lists of recommendations created by experts who are remote from students and the leadership role of the school staff is not easily resolved, and may result in the staff's hesitating or refusing to get involved in renewal efforts. If a school staff cannot identify its own priorities for improving student learning, it is unlikely that it can muster the talent and commitment necessary for sustained action to implement recommendations advanced by remote sources.

Rather than give educators in public schools recipes for what should be done, we think it is crucial for robust dialogues to take place in individual schools—discussions and debates that lead to identification and solution of significant problems. To initiate these professional dialogues that are central to the renewal process, we suggest that the principal gather the school staff to consider the following premises.

A "premise," as used here, is an assertion about the practical nature of school environments. If considered, premises may lead to decisions and appropriate actions by educators to alter those conditions that hinder marginal students' learning. The interrelated premises that we advance form a conceptual base intended to spark constructive dialogue and encourage positive action for bringing about desired changes. Clearly, not all possible premises for resolving the persistent problems of marginality can be included here. The list would start to resemble the overly detailed blueprints for action that often hinder local initiative and limit staff decision making about educational goals of their schools. Instead, we selected a manageable number of pertinent premises that our work in public schools suggests are constructively related to preparing the school environment for improvement. In particular, the premises are aimed at making the environment more responsive to marginal students.

We wish to promote a spirited dialogue in schools that are striving for renewal. From a discussion of these premises, and of others that teachers and administrators might add, the necessary and personalized agenda for assisting greater numbers of public school students to learn more may be defined and then implemented.

PREMISES FOR DIALOGUE AND ACTION

The following premises serve as a practical starting point for considering and resolving the problems of marginal students.

- It is possible to create varied educational conditions so that all learners reach similar high levels of academic achievement. In particular, it is possible to increase learning for marginal students without decreasing learning for currently successful students.

- Every student runs the risk of experiencing temporary or perhaps permanent marginality, which is disconnection from productive learning in school.

- Marginality does not always result from the learner's characteristics. Rather, it often develops from low-quality interactions between the learner and the environment. By looking closely at these interactions, it is possible to gain an understanding of why many learners become marginal.

- Students who are forced to the margins of school can provide important information about how to improve curriculum, instruction, and organization, because each day they experience the environmental constraints that stymie their efforts to learn.

- Hardening patterns of marginal behavior do not readily dissolve, because young people and educators alike experience pressures that hinder their ability to change the unproductive relationship between the marginal learner and the school environment.

- Teachers' interactions with marginal students are influenced by unnecessary regularities—routine or habitual ways of organizing and conducting classroom activities—that are seldom identified, discussed, or changed.

- Schools contain conditions of curriculum, instruction, and organization that may hinder learning for some students. These conditions can be replaced by means that provide all students with equal access to a quality education. In this sense, the school environment is both a source that contributes to marginal behavior and a force that can be adjusted to improve learning.

- Each school develops a unique culture in response to particular internal and external constituencies. For this reason, there is no single approach to improving the learning of marginal students. Each school needs to assess its own educational resources and practices while developing solutions to the problem of marginal students based on its strengths.

- Several of the necessary conditions for effective learning are schoolwide and are not produced simply by individual teachers working alone. The principal and teachers working in concert in the single school can create the capacity for improvement necessary for increasing marginal students' learning.

- Homes and schools can join together to create powerful interventions to help students who have a history of failure become successful learners. Cooperation and collaboration between parents and teachers affect students' attitudes and the skills they apply to learning. Few students are beyond the help that can be provided when home and school work together over time.

- To bring about a significant improvement in the educational effectiveness of a school requires considerable effort and time. It is estimated that the time needed to affect significant and lasting change is typically about five to seven years.

Proposals for reform often make striking, exuberant appearances, flashing with promise and potential. Those proposals that can be discerned in schools at a later point seldom retain their promised power. Given this history, it seems necessary that preliminary work, more fundamental than installing a new program or recommendation, must be done to prepare the school for improvement.

For marginal behavior to decline, the student's relationship with the learning environment has to improve. Conversely, for learning environments to become more responsive, educators' roles and responsibilities with marginal students have to be redefined. To guide this renewal process, premises about the practical possibilities of schools are advanced for discussion by school staffs. The premises have not been elaborated with research and rationale here, partly because the premises bring together themes from various chapters of this book and partly because they are intended to raise questions that educators have to ask of themselves and of one another.

National and state legislation, central-office mandates, or principal directives may help set a context for changing faculty behavior and improving the local school, but they are not in themselves sufficient to sustain the commitment needed for faculty to develop and maintain different ways of teaching or relating with students. For example, to change habitual teaching practices that are not working with marginal students, each teacher has to reflect on alternate views of how he or she could engage with these learners. As teachers reconsider the way they think about and act toward marginal students, a productive tension will gradually mount. This is a tension between existing practices seen increasingly as unsatis-factory or even unworthy and envisioned practices seen increasingly as possible and necessary.

The premises, then, serve as conceptual tools that thrust before a school staff the full challenge of the responsibility to help all youngsters become successful learners. The premises can function as an intellectual scalpel that cuts painfully close to the heart and conscience of educators not accustomed to judging themselves against the standard of all children learning. For the many educators who are committed to assuring that all youth learn, consideration of these premises will provide a welcome forum to convince others of their obligations and to show skeptics how they may reach and teach marginal students. It is from this group of professional educators that we expect to find the leadership needed for the renewal of schools.

It can become discouraging to realize that what professional educators and others want from American schools is often more envisioned than practiced. Yet we are optimistic about the progress that can be made by educators working in their local schools to increase learning for those students who for too long have not experienced academic success. Also, we are confident that the concern for marginal students will catch the imagination of educators. Their innovative thinking and constructive action can stimulate reforms that will empower public schools to provide marginal students with a responsive environment for learning. Only by attending to marginal students is it possible to preserve a system of public education committed to equal access and quality learning for all children and youth.